THE FIRST-TIME REAL ESTATE INVESTOR'S GUIDE TO BIG RETURNS

LORENZO L. **SELLERS**

Published by Lorenzo L. Sellers, in the United States of America.

Copyright © 2024 Lorenzo L. Sellers

All rights reserved. No part of this publication may be reproduced, distributed, or transmitted in any form or by any means, including photocopying, recording, or other electronic or mechanical methods, without the prior written permission of the publisher, except in the case of brief quotations embodied in critical reviews and certain other noncommercial uses permitted by copyright law.

ISBN: 9798336234459

DISCLAIMER AND/OR LEGAL NOTICES:

While all attempts have been made to verify information provided in this publication, neither the Author nor the Publisher assumes an responsibility for errors, inaccuracies, or omissions. Any slights of people or organizations are unintentional.

This publication is not intended for use as a source of legal or accounting advice. The Publisher wants to stress that the information contained herein may be subject to varying state and/or local laws or regulations.

The reader of this publication assumes responsibility for the use of these materials and information. Adherence to all applicable laws and regulations, including advertising and all other aspects of doing business in the United States or any other jurisdiction is the sole responsibility of the reader. The Author and publisher assume no responsibility or liability whatsoever on behalf of any reader of these materials.

This book is dedicated to the hustlers, the dreamers, and the go-getters who refuse to settle for anything less than greatness. To those who see opportunity where others see obstacles, who get up after every fall, and who are never satisfied with just good enough.

To my mentors, who taught me the ropes and showed me that success is earned, not given. To my family, whose love and support are the foundation of everything I do. And to the next generation of real estate moguls—may you take these lessons, build on them, and create legacies that will stand the test of time.

This is for you. Keep pushing, keep striving, and never forget that the sky is not the limit—it's just the beginning.

CONTENTS

INTRODUCTION *1*

PART I : LAYING THE **FOUNDATION**

The Journey Begins: Understanding Real Estate Investment *7*

Setting Your Goals: Defining Success in Real Estate *13*

Market Mastery: Researching and Selecting the Right Market *23*

Financing Fundamentals: Exploring Your Investment Options *33*

PART II : TAKING **ACTION**

Building Your Team: Assembling the Right Experts *45*

Property Hunt: Finding the Perfect Investment Opportunity *55*

Crunching the Numbers: Analyzing Potential Deals *79*

The Art of Negotiation: Securing the Best Deal *87*

PART III : CLOSING & **MANAGING**

The Due Diligence Dance: Avoiding Common Pitfalls *97*

Closing the Deal: Navigating the Final Steps *105*

Property Management 101: Ensuring a Smooth Operation *113*

Maximizing Returns: Strategies for Profit Growth *119*

PART IV : EXPANDING & **REFLECTING**

Overcoming Challenges: What to Do When Things Go Wrong *127*

Building a Portfolio: Expanding Your Investment Horizons *137*

Long-Term Vision: Planning for Future Success *145*

Reflecting on the Journey: Lessons Learned and Next Steps *153*

The Journey Continues: Your Next Steps in Real Estate Success *161*

Appendix: Resources and Tools for Real Estate Professionals *165*

Acknowledgement *171*

INTRODUCTION

Alright, let's get real for a second. You've heard the stories, seen the headlines, maybe even watched a few too many episodes of those real estate reality shows. You've got a gut feeling that real estate could be your ticket to something bigger—something better. But where do you start? How do you turn that spark of an idea into a full-blown success story?

Let me break it down for you: real estate is not just for the rich and famous. It's not just for the pros who've been in the game for decades. It's for you. Yes, you—the person who's hungry, who's ready to hustle, and who knows there's a better way to build a future than clocking in and out of a 9-to-5 for the next 40 years.

This book is your backstage pass to the real estate world. It's the guide I wish I had when I was getting started—no fluff, no BS, just straight-up, actionable advice that'll take you from rookie to rockstar investor.

This book is your entry point into the world of real estate investing. It's not just another "how-to" guide filled with generic advice and complicated jargon. Instead, it's a step-by-step blueprint designed specifically for people like you—those who are eager to break into real estate but might feel overwhelmed by the complexities, uncertainties, and risks associated with it.

Why Real Estate? Because It Works.

Here's the deal: real estate isn't some pie-in-the-sky dream. It's not a get-rich-quick scheme either. It's real, it's tangible, and it works. You can see it, touch it, and—if you play your cards right—profit from it. The beauty of real estate is that it's a game anyone can play, and guess what? You don't need to be a financial genius to win. You just need the right strategy, the right mindset, and the willingness to roll up your sleeves and get to work.

Let's be clear: I'm not promising you overnight riches. I'm promising you a path—a proven path—that, if you follow it, will lead you to financial freedom. And along the way, you'll learn, you'll grow, and you'll gain something way more valuable than money: confidence. Confidence in your ability to make smart decisions, to weather the ups and downs, and to build something that lasts.

Taking the First Step: It's Go Time

Look, I get it. Starting anything new can be scary. You might be wondering, "What if I mess up? What if I pick the wrong property? What if this whole thing goes south?" But here's the thing: the only way to truly fail is to do nothing. Every successful investor you've ever heard of started where you are right now—unsure, a little nervous, but ready to take action.

This book is your cheat sheet. It's going to guide you through every step of the process, from understanding the basics of real estate to closing your first deal and beyond. I'm not just going to tell you what to do—I'm going to show you how to do it, with real-world examples, insider tips, and strategies that actually work.

Real Estate: The Ultimate Power Move

Why should you dive into real estate? Because it's the ultimate power move. It's about more than just making money—it's about taking control of your life, your future, and your freedom. Real estate gives you options. It lets you build wealth on your terms, whether that means creating passive income, securing your retirement, or flipping your way to financial independence.

But let's not sugarcoat it: real estate isn't always easy. There will be challenges, setbacks, and moments when you might question why you even started. But trust me, if you stick with it, if you stay focused, the rewards are worth it. And the best part? You're not going through it alone. I've been there, and I'm here to walk you through it, step by step.

Building Your Legacy Starts Now

This isn't just about buying a property or two—it's about building a legacy. It's about creating something that will outlast you, something that can provide for your family for generations. This book is your blueprint for that legacy. We're going to cover everything—how to spot a good deal, how to negotiate like a pro, how to manage your properties, and most importantly, how to think like an investor.

So, are you ready? Ready to turn that spark into a blazing fire of success? Ready to step into the world of real estate and claim your piece of the pie? The journey starts right here, right now. All you have to do is take that first step, and I promise you, the view from the top is worth every bit of the climb.

Let's crush it together.. The world of real estate is waiting for you—and your time starts now.

Lorenzo L. Sellers

PART I
LAYING THE **FOUNDATION**

THE JOURNEY BEGINS: UNDERSTANDING REAL **ESTATE INVESTMENT**

Real estate? It's the OG path to wealth creation. Whether you're buying your first home or snapping up commercial properties, real estate is your ticket to financial security and big returns. But before you dive in headfirst, you've got to nail down the basics—the "why" and the "how" that'll guide you on your way to the top.

This chapter is your launchpad. Whether real estate has never crossed your mind as an investment or you're already buzzing with curiosity, this is where you'll get the lowdown on why real estate is the ultimate wealth-building machine. We'll break down how it stacks up against other investments and arm you with the know-how you need to kick off your journey with confidence. Buckle up—this is where it all begins.

Seriously, Why Real Estate?

Real estate investing isn't just about owning property; it's about leveraging that property to create wealth. Unlike stocks or bonds, real estate is a tangible asset—you can see it, touch it, and improve it. This tangibility provides a sense of security and control that other investment types often lack.

But what makes real estate truly compelling as an investment?

Here are a few key reasons:

Multiple Income Streams: Real estate is like a Swiss Army knife for generating income. You've got rental properties bringing in steady cash flow, property values appreciating over time, and plenty of other money-making moves like house flipping, short-term rentals, and commercial leasing. It's a buffet of opportunities, and every option is a potential payday.

Tax Benefits: Real estate investors get some sweet tax perks—think deductions on mortgage interest, property taxes, insurance, and even depreciation. These benefits can seriously slash your taxable income and give your overall return on investment a nice little boost. It's like getting a bonus just for being smart with your money!

Leverage: With real estate, you can leverage other people's money—usually through mortgages or loans—to control a valuable asset. This means you can get into the game with a relatively small upfront investment and watch your potential returns multiply. It's like using someone else's cash to build your empire.

Appreciation: Over time, real estate tends to go up in value, especially if you pick the right spots. This appreciation can lead to serious long-term gains, especially when you add in the income you're already pulling in from the property. It's like your investment is working double-time for you.

Inflation Hedge: Real estate is your inflation-proof sidekick. As the cost of living goes up, so do property values and rental incomes, keeping your purchasing power strong and your wealth protected. It's like having a built-in shield against inflation.

Types of Real Estate Investments

Real estate is a broad field with many different types of investments to consider. Understanding the various options will help you identify the best starting point for your journey.
Here are some of the most common types of real estate investments:

Residential Properties: This is where most investors kick off their journey. We're talking single-family homes, condos, townhouses, and multi-family properties like duplexes or apartment buildings. It's the go-to starting point because it's accessible and, let's face it, everyone knows a thing or two about the housing market. A solid foundation for building your real estate empire!

Commercial Properties: Think big! We're talking office buildings, retail spaces, warehouses, and industrial spots. These properties can deliver higher returns than your average residential investment, but they also come with bigger price tags and a need for serious management skills. High stakes, high rewards—if you're ready to play in the big leagues.

Rental Properties: Buying rental properties? Now you're building your own cash machine! Whether it's residential or commercial, the goal is simple: rent them out and watch the steady income roll in. Plus, you're not just earning cash flow—you're sitting on an asset that could appreciate over time. It's a double win!

Flipping Houses: The game is simple: buy undervalued or fixer-upper properties, work your magic, and sell them for a sweet profit. But it's not for the faint of heart. You need a sharp eye for value, killer project management skills, and a deep understanding of the local market. Get it right, and you're cashing in big time.

Real Estate Investment Trusts (REITs): REITs let you invest in real estate without owning property. You buy shares in a company that handles the assets, offering you diversification, liquidity, and potential dividends—ideal for those wanting real estate exposure minus the landlord duties.

Vacation Rentals: Short-term rentals through platforms like Airbnb or VRBO? Cha-ching! These vacation spots can pull in way more cash than long-term rentals, especially if you're in a hot tourist area. But here's the catch: you'll have more tenant turnover and a bit more hands-on management. Worth it? Totally—if you're ready for the hustle.

Land Investment: Oh, you're going full-on visionary! It's a bold move—risky, sure, but it could pay off big time. Land is like a blank canvas, waiting for the next Picasso (that's you) to turn it into a masterpiece. If you pick the right spot—an area that's about to blow up—your investment could skyrocket in value. Develop it, lease it, or just watch the value climb. High risk, high reward, my friend.

The Investment Mindset

Before we jump into the nitty-gritty, let's talk mindset. Because if you're going to play this game, you need to play it right. Real estate isn't about quick wins—it's about smart moves. You need patience, persistence, and the kind of determination that doesn't quit when things get tough (and trust me, they will). Here are some key mindsets to adopt:

Patience: Real estate is generally not a get-rich-quick scheme. It requires patience and a long-term perspective. Property values don't skyrocket overnight, and building a portfolio takes time and effort.

Persistence: The path to success in real estate is rarely smooth. There will be challenges—difficult tenants, market downturns, unexpected repairs—but successful investors persist through these difficulties, learning from their experiences and adapting their strategies.

Continuous Learning: The best investors? They never stop learning. The market is always changing, and if you're not keeping up, you're falling behind. So, get ready to dig into books, podcasts, seminars—whatever it takes to stay sharp.

Risk Management: Real estate isn't risk-free. Again, there will be challenges—market downturns, tough tenants, deals that fall through. But here's the thing: Every challenge is an opportunity in disguise. The key is to manage that risk, learn from every experience, and come out stronger on the other side.

Networking: Real estate is all about the people you know. Your network is your net worth. Surround yourself with the right crew —agents, brokers, contractors, property managers, and fellow investors—and you'll open doors you never even knew existed. These connections aren't just contacts; they're your ticket to top-notch advice, killer opportunities, and the support you need to crush it in this game.

The First Steps: Getting Started

Alright, you're pumped up, you're motivated—now what? Now we take that energy and turn it into action. Here's your playbook for getting started:

Set Clear Goals: What do you want out of this? Passive income? Long-term appreciation? A mix of both? Get clear on your goals because they'll guide every move you make.

Do Your Homework: Knowledge is power. Read, watch, listen

—absorb everything you can about the real estate market. This book is your launchpad, but don't stop here. Keep learning, keep growing.

Check Your Finances: How much cash do you have to work with? What's your credit score? Can you qualify for a mortgage? Know your numbers, because they'll dictate what kind of properties you can go after.

Start Small, Think Big: Your first investment doesn't need to be a mansion in the Hamptons. Start with something manageable—a single-family home, a duplex, maybe even a condo. Get your feet wet, learn the ropes, and build from there.

Make a Plan: This isn't a fly-by-night operation. You need a solid game plan—what you're buying, how you're financing it, and what your exit strategy is. Write it down, map it out, and stick to it.

Take the Leap, Take Action: This is where most people freeze. They get stuck in analysis paralysis, too afraid to make the first move. Don't be that person. Trust your research, trust your plan, and take the leap. You'll learn more from doing than from a thousand hours of reading.

Your Journey Begins Here

This is it. You've got the motivation, the mindset, and the basics to start your real estate journey. The path won't always be easy, but it will be worth it. Remember, every real estate mogul started with their first property. The difference between them and everyone else? They didn't just dream about it—they did it.

Now it's your turn. Your journey begins here, and I'll be with you every step of the way. So, let's go make some deals, build some wealth, and create a legacy that'll last for generations. The world of real estate is waiting for you—let's get started.

SETTING YOUR GOALS: DEFINING SUCCESS IN **REAL ESTATE**

Alright, folks, let's get one thing straight: you wouldn't start a road trip without knowing where you're going, right? You don't just hop in the car, crank up your favorite tunes, and drive aimlessly into the sunset. Well, maybe you do, but that's a different story. The point is, in real estate investing, having a clear destination—aka your goals—is the key to not getting lost in the middle of nowhere with no gas station in sight.

Setting goals isn't just for overachievers who have their whole lives planned out on color-coded spreadsheets (although, kudos to them). It's for anyone who wants to make serious money and avoid the whole "oops, I bought a house that's sinking into the ground" scenario. Goals give you direction, they give you purpose, and most importantly, they give you bragging rights when you achieve them.

Why Goal Setting Matters

Imagine you're at an all-you-can-eat buffet, but there's a catch: you have to plan your meal before you even see the food. If you don't, you end up with a plate full of kale and quinoa while your friend has a mountain of fried chicken and chocolate cake. Not cool, right?

Setting goals in real estate is kind of like planning your buffet attack. You need to know what you want before you start piling stuff on your plate, or in this case, before you start buying properties left and right. Goals help you figure out what's going to satisfy your appetite for success (and your bank account) without leaving you feeling stuffed with regret.

Here's why goals are your best friend:

Clarity of Purpose: Goals give you a reason to get out of bed in the morning and do something other than binge-watch Netflix. They remind you why you're investing in real estate in the first place—whether it's to make a ton of money, retire early, or just prove to your in-laws that you're not totally crazy.

Decision-Making Framework: Goals are like the friend who tells you when you're about to make a bad decision. "Does this property fit with your plan, or are you just buying it because you love the wallpaper?" Goals keep you focused and stop you from making impulsive decisions that could cost you big time.

Measurable Progress: How do you know if you're winning if you don't keep score? Goals let you track your progress and give yourself a pat on the back (or a kick in the pants) as needed.

Focus and Prioritization: Real estate is full of shiny objects. Goals help you ignore the distractions and focus on what really matters—like making money, duh.

Accountability: Goals keep you honest. If you set a goal and don't achieve it, well, that's on you. But if you do achieve it, you get to celebrate like a champ.

Types of Real Estate Investment Goals

Now, let's talk about the different types of goals you might want to set, depending on what kind of real estate superhero you want to be. Think of these as the superpowers you're aiming to develop:

Cash Flow Goals: This is the goal for you if you want to have money rolling in every month like clockwork. You're the kind of investor who wants your properties to be cash cows, not cash pits. The goal here is to find properties that generate steady, predictable income—enough to cover your expenses and leave you with a nice pile of cash at the end of the month.

Appreciation Goals: If you're more of a long-term thinker, this might be your jam. You're looking for properties that are going to increase in value over time. It's like buying low and selling high, but with real estate instead of those Beanie Babies you've been hoarding since the 90s.

Portfolio Growth Goals: Maybe you want to be the next real estate mogul, owning properties all over town—or even all over the country. This goal is all about building a big, diverse portfolio of properties. Think of it as your real estate empire. The more properties you own, the more control you have over your financial destiny.

Tax Efficiency Goals: Who doesn't love paying less in taxes? If you're smart, you'll set goals that help you maximize the tax benefits of owning real estate. Things like depreciation, 1031 exchanges, and other tax-saving strategies can save you a boatload of money—money you can use to buy more properties, of course.

Wealth Building Goals: This is the big picture goal—the one where you build serious wealth over time. You're in it for the long haul, accumulating equity, reducing debt, and reinvesting your profits to grow your portfolio. It's like playing Monopoly, but with real houses and no annoying paper money

Lifestyle Goals: Maybe you're not in it just for the money. Maybe you want to use real estate to fund a specific lifestyle —like retiring early, traveling the world, or just spending more time with your family. Real estate can help you achieve those lifestyle goals, but you've got to be clear about what you want.

How to Set SMART Goals

Okay, time to get down to business. When setting goals, you've got to be SMART about it. No, I don't mean wearing glasses and using big words. I'm talking about setting goals that are:

- **Specific:** Be clear about what you want. "Make money in real estate" isn't specific enough. Try something like, "Buy two rental properties that generate $2,000 a month in cash flow by the end of next year."

- **Measurable:** If you can't measure it, how do you know if you've achieved it? Make sure your goals have numbers attached so you can track your progress.

- **Achievable:** Let's be real—you're probably not going to own 50 properties by the end of the year if you're just starting out. Set goals that are challenging but doable.

- **Relevant:** Your goals should make sense for where you are in your life and career. If your goal is to retire in five years, buying a fixer-upper that's going to take you ten years to flip might not be the best idea.

- **Time-Bound:** Give yourself a deadline. Goals without

deadlines are just wishes. And we're not in the business of making wishes—we're in the business of making things happen.

Aligning Real Estate Goals with Life Goals

Let's get a little deep for a moment. Real estate isn't just about making money (okay, maybe it mostly is, but bear with me). It's also about aligning your investments with your overall life goals. What do you really want out of life? How can real estate help you get there?

Think about the big picture. Are you investing to create security for your family? To fund your dream retirement? To become the next big thing in real estate? Whatever your life goals are, your real estate goals should support them. Otherwise, you're just spinning your wheels.

Take time to reflect on what you truly want from life and how real estate can help you achieve it. For example:

- **Family Security:** If your primary goal is to provide for your family, you might focus on building a portfolio that generates reliable income and can be passed down to future generations.

- **Early Retirement:** If you dream of retiring early, your goals might involve creating enough passive income to cover your living expenses and give you the freedom to leave your job.

- **Financial Independence:** If your goal is financial independence, you might prioritize cash flow goals that allow you to live off your real estate income, giving you the freedom to pursue other passions.

- **Philanthropy:** If giving back is important to you, real estate can be a way to fund your charitable activities, whether by donating rental income, providing affordable housing, or using profits to support causes you care about.

By aligning your real estate goals with your life goals, you ensure that your investment strategy is not just about making money but about creating the life you want.

Breaking Down Long-Term Goals into Actionable Steps

Once you've set your long-term goals, it's essential to break them down into smaller, actionable steps. This process helps you avoid feeling overwhelmed and allows you to make steady progress. Here's how to do it:

Identify Milestones: Break your big goals into smaller milestones. Each milestone is a mini-goal that gets you closer to the big one. For example, if your goal is to acquire ten rental properties in ten years, a milestone might be purchasing your first property within the next year.

Create a Timeline: Give each milestone a deadline. This keeps you moving forward and prevents procrastination.

Develop an Action Plan: For each milestone, write down the specific steps you need to take. This might include things like researching markets, finding financing, or stalking Zillow like it's your job (because it kind of is).

Monitor Progress: Check in with yourself regularly to see how you're doing. If you're falling behind, adjust your plan. If you're ahead of schedule, give yourself a high-five.

Stay Flexible: Real estate is like life—things don't always go according to plan. Be ready to pivot if necessary. Just because you've got a plan doesn't mean you can't change it if something better comes along.

Your Roadmap to Success

So there you have it—the secret sauce to setting goals that will make you a real estate celebrity (maybe you'll wind up as one the sharks on Shark Tank). Goals aren't just for people who like to write in planners and cross things off to-do lists (although, again, props to them). They're for anyone who wants to make serious money, build a real estate empire, or just have more control over their life.

Remember, the road to success in real estate is a long one, but with clear goals, you've got your GPS set. Now all you have to do is follow the directions, avoid the potholes, and keep your eyes on the prize.

As you continue through this book, keep your goals in mind. Let them guide your learning, shape your strategies, and inspire you to take action. Real estate investing is not just about acquiring properties; it's about creating the life you want. With your goals as your roadmap, you're well on your way to turning your real estate dreams into reality.

A Personal Story: How One Client's Goal Setting Transformed Their Real Estate Journey

Meet Jennifer. When she first walked into my office, she had that spark—a mix of excitement and nerves, ready to dive into real estate but unsure where to start. Like a lot of first-time investors, Jennifer had some cash and a desire to make it work for her, but no clear strategy. She was overwhelmed by the endless possibilities: Should she go for a rental property? Maybe try her hand at flipping? Commercial real estate, perhaps? With so many options, it felt like she was spinning her wheels.

So, I asked her one question that changed everything: "What do you really want to achieve?"

At first, her answer was broad, the kind of response I've heard a hundred times. "I want to make money. I want to be smart with my investment."

But I knew there was more to her story. As we talked, Jennifer opened up about her real motivation. She's a single mom, working long hours, barely seeing her two young kids. What she truly wanted wasn't just money—it was freedom. The kind of financial freedom that would let her spend more time with her children and pursue a passion project she'd put on the back burner for years.

That's when the light bulb went off. Jennifer didn't just need an investment; she needed a plan, a clear path to financial freedom. Her goal became crystal clear: generate enough passive income in five years to cut back on work and start living life on her terms.

With that goal in mind, we got to work. Instead of chasing every shiny object in real estate, we focused on a strategy that aligned with her vision. We found a small multi-family property—a duplex in a great neighborhood with strong rental demand. It wasn't flashy, but it was exactly what she needed to get started. The rental income from one unit covered most of her mortgage, while the second unit gave her that extra cash flow to start making moves.

Fast forward a few years, and Jennifer's life looks completely different. She didn't just stop at one property; she kept building. Reinvesting her profits, she picked up a second property, then a third, each time with a clear focus on her endgame. And you know what? She hit her goal. Actually, she crushed it. Jennifer left her full-time job, launched her own business, and spends more time with her kids than she ever imagined possible.

Jennifer's journey is the perfect example of why setting clear goals is non-negotiable in real estate.

It's not just about buying properties or making money—it's about defining what success looks like for you and going all in to make it happen. For Jennifer, it wasn't about getting rich quick; it was about creating a life where she could be there for her kids and pursue her passions. With her goals locked in, she turned what was once a dream into a reality.

In the world of real estate, it's easy to get lost in the details. But when you have a clear goal, like Jennifer did, everything else falls into place. It's not just about the properties; it's about building the life you want, one smart investment at a time.

MARKET MASTERY: RESEARCHING AND **SELECTING THE RIGHT MARKET**

Alright, so you've set your goals, you're pumped up, and you're ready to dive into the world of real estate. But hold on a second, champ—you can't just throw a dart at a map and start buying properties. Unless, of course, you want to end up with a plot of land in the middle of nowhere where the only inhabitants are tumbleweeds and a lone coyote.

No, my friend, picking the right market is where the real magic happens. This is where fortunes are made—or lost. It's like picking a restaurant on a Saturday night: you don't want to end up at some sketchy joint where the "special of the day" has been special for the last three weeks.

So, how do you choose the perfect market? How do you find that sweet spot where the grass is green, the people are happy, and the real estate gods are smiling down on you? Let's dive in and find out.

The Myth of the Perfect Market

First things first, let's bust a myth: there's no such thing as the perfect market. That's like looking for the perfect partner who loves everything you do, never argues, and always agrees to your dinner plans. (Spoiler alert: they don't exist.)

Every market has its pros and cons. The key is finding a market that aligns with your goals, your budget, and your risk tolerance. It's about finding a place where the numbers make sense, the future looks bright, and the locals won't chase you out with pitchforks when they find out you're an investor.

Market Research: The Fun Part (Seriously, It Can Be Fun)

Now, I know what you're thinking: "Research? Ugh, that sounds boring." But trust me, market research is like detective work, except you get to keep the treasure at the end. And who doesn't want to feel like Sherlock Holmes with a real estate license?

Here's how to do it without falling asleep:

Get to Know the Neighborhoods: Start by scoping out different neighborhoods within your target market. Are they up-and-coming, or are they on a slow slide into mediocrity? Are there coffee shops, trendy boutiques, and artisanal donut shops popping up? Or is the local grocery store still selling milk in glass bottles? The vibe of a neighborhood can tell you a lot about its potential.

Check the Numbers: Time to get nerdy. Look at the stats—median home prices, rental yields, vacancy rates, and how they've changed over the last few years. If numbers make your eyes glaze over, remember that these are the digits that could make or break your investment. It's like checking the calories on a donut—important if you care about your future (or your waistline).

Future Growth Prospects: Is the market growing or shrinking? Are people flocking to the area like it's the next big thing, or are they leaving faster than you can say "foreclosure"? Look at population trends, job growth, and any planned developments. A new school, a shopping mall, or a tech hub could mean big things for property values.

Local Economy: What's driving the local economy? Is it a one-trick pony that could collapse if the main employer goes belly-up? Or is it diverse and thriving, with multiple industries pumping money into the area? The stronger and more varied the economy, the safer your investment.

Crime Rates: Nobody wants to invest in a place where the biggest growth industry is the local prison. Check out crime rates, because safety is a big deal for renters and buyers alike. You want a market where people feel secure leaving their doors unlocked (okay, maybe not that secure, but you get the point).

School Districts: Good schools are like the Holy Grail of real estate. Families will pay top dollar to be in the right district, so look for areas with highly rated schools. Even if you don't have kids, your future buyers or tenants might, and they care —a lot.

Infrastructure and Amenities: What's the traffic like? Are there public transportation options? How about parks, shopping centers, and restaurants? A market with good infrastructure and plenty of amenities is more attractive to renters and buyers, which means more money in your pocket.

Regulations and Taxes: Finally, don't forget to check out the local regulations and taxes. Some places are more landlord-friendly than others, and property taxes can vary wildly. You don't want to find out after you've bought a property that the local government is planning to triple property taxes to fund a new pet project.

Hot, Warm, or Cold: How to Categorize Markets

Once you've done your detective work, it's time to categorize the markets. Think of them like Goldilocks and the Three Bears—some markets are too hot, some are too cold, and some are just right.

Hot Markets: These are the markets everyone's talking about. Prices are skyrocketing, bidding wars are common, and the risk of overpaying is high. Hot markets can be tempting, but they're also volatile. You've got to be quick on your feet, and you need deep pockets. Think of them as the Kardashians of real estate—high-profile, but not always worth the drama.

Cold Markets: These markets are the exact opposite. They're stagnant, with little to no growth, and properties can sit on the market for ages. Cold markets might seem like a bargain, but they're often cheap for a reason. Unless you're a master at turning things around, you might end up stuck with a lemon.

Warm Markets: These are the sweet spots. They're not making headlines, but they're stable, with steady growth and solid returns. Warm markets are like that reliable friend who's always there for you—maybe not the life of the party, but dependable and low-maintenance.

The Goldilocks Zone: Finding "Just Right"

So how do you find a market that's just right? Here are a few tips:

Look for Undervalued Areas: Sometimes, the best markets are the ones that haven't been discovered yet. Look for neighborhoods or cities that are on the brink of gentrification or development. If you can get in before everyone else does, you could ride the wave of appreciation.

Balance Risk and Reward: Don't get caught up in the hype of a hot market unless you're prepared for the risk. At the same time, don't play it so safe that you miss out on potential gains. Find a market that offers a good balance—decent returns with manageable risk.

Listen to the Locals: Sometimes, the best information comes from the people who live there. Talk to local real estate agents, shop owners, and residents. They'll give you the scoop on what's really happening in the area—and whether it's worth your investment.

Diversify: Don't put all your eggs in one basket. Consider investing in multiple markets to spread out your risk. That way, if one market cools off, you've still got others that are performing well.

Tools and Resources for Market Research

In today's digital age, you have access to a wealth of tools and resources that can help you research and analyze real estate markets. Here are some of the most valuable ones:

Online Real Estate Platforms: Websites like Zillow, Realtor.com, and Redfin offer detailed property listings, market trends, and neighborhood data. Use these platforms to compare prices, track appreciation rates, and monitor rental rates.

Economic Reports: Government agencies and research firms publish economic reports that provide valuable insights into market conditions. Look for reports from the U.S. Census Bureau, the Bureau of Labor Statistics, and local economic development agencies.

Local Real Estate Boards: Many cities have local real estate boards or associations that publish market data, including property sales, rental rates, and market trends. These organizations are also great sources of networking and educational opportunities.

Networking with Local Experts: Connect with local real estate agents, property managers, and other investors in your target market. These professionals can provide firsthand insights into market conditions, neighborhoods, and investment opportunities.

News and Media: Stay informed about local news and developments that could impact the real estate market. Subscribe to local newspapers, follow industry blogs, and join online forums where investors share insights and experiences.

Social Media and Online Communities: Join real estate investment groups on social media platforms like Facebook, LinkedIn, and Reddit. These communities are great places to ask questions, share experiences, and learn from other investors.

Making the Final Decision

After conducting thorough research, it's time to make your decision. Choosing the right market requires a balance of data-driven analysis and intuition. Trust the research, but also listen to your instincts. If a market checks all the boxes but doesn't feel right, it might be worth reconsidering.

Remember, there's no such thing as a perfect market. Every

market has its strengths and weaknesses. The key is to find a market that aligns with your investment goals, risk tolerance, and long-term strategy. Once you've made your decision, commit to it, and dive in with confidence.

The Market Is Your Playground

At the end of the day, picking the right market is a mix of art and science. You've got to do your homework, trust your instincts, and be willing to take a calculated risk. But when you find that perfect market—the one that's just right for your goals—you'll know it. The numbers will make sense, the future will look bright, and you'll be ready to make your move.

So go out there and find your market. Explore, analyze, and get ready to make some serious money. Remember, the real estate jungle is full of opportunities—if you know where to look.

And when you find that hidden gem, don't forget to send me a postcard from your yacht.

A Personal Story: How One Client Mastered Market Selection in Virginia

Let me tell you about a client of mine, David. David was a seasoned IT manager in his late forties with a clear vision of his next big move: real estate investment. Living in Virginia, he had always been intrigued by the potential of real estate but was unsure where to start. Should he invest locally in the high-priced Northern Virginia market, or look for opportunities in more affordable areas? The choice felt overwhelming, and he wasn't sure how to make the best decision.

David came to me with a clear goal—he wanted to build a real estate portfolio that would generate passive income and eventually allow him to retire early. But he wasn't interested in just any market; he needed one that would offer steady growth and a good return on investment.

Our first task was to understand his priorities. David wanted a market with strong rental demand, moderate property prices, and room for appreciation. He wasn't interested in the ultra-competitive Northern Virginia market, where high entry costs made it difficult to find properties with good cash flow. Instead, he was open to exploring other parts of Virginia where his investment could stretch further.

We began by researching different regions in Virginia. We looked at cities like Richmond, Virginia Beach, and Charlottesville. Each of these markets had unique characteristics and potential. Richmond had a growing job market and affordable properties, Virginia Beach was known for its strong rental demand due to tourism and military presence, and Charlottesville offered a mix of historical charm and a vibrant university community.

To narrow down the options, we analyzed key market data: rental yields, property appreciation rates, economic indicators, and local infrastructure developments. I encouraged David to take a closer look at these markets not just through data, but by experiencing them firsthand.

David decided to visit Richmond and Virginia Beach. He spent a weekend in each city, meeting with local real estate agents, exploring neighborhoods, and getting a feel for the local lifestyle. In Richmond, he found a city with a rich history, a burgeoning food scene, and a rapidly growing tech sector. The property prices were reasonable, and the rental demand was strong due to the influx of young professionals and families.

Virginia Beach, on the other hand, offered the allure of coastal living and a stable rental market driven by its military base and tourism. The property prices were slightly higher than in Richmond, but the rental income potential from vacation rentals was a significant draw.

After his visits, David was particularly impressed by Richmond. The city's combination of affordability, growth potential, and a thriving cultural scene resonated with him. He could see the city's development trajectory and felt confident in its ability to provide both steady rental income and long-term appreciation.

David made his first investment in a well-located multi-family property in Richmond. The property was situated in a neighborhood undergoing revitalization, and its proximity to downtown and local amenities made it highly attractive to renters. The investment paid off quickly, with strong rental income and noticeable appreciation in property value within the first year.

Buoyed by his success, David continued to expand his portfolio in Richmond. He reinvested the profits from his initial property into additional multi-family units and single-family homes, each time selecting properties that aligned with his growth strategy.

David's experience is a testament to the importance of thorough market research and firsthand experience. By carefully evaluating different markets and trusting his instincts, David was able to select a Virginia market that met his investment goals and provided the foundation for a successful real estate career.

In the world of real estate, finding the right market is crucial. David's story shows that with the right approach—combining data analysis with personal exploration—you can find a market that not only meets your investment criteria but also aligns with your long-term vision. For David, Richmond became more than just a location; it was the key to unlocking his financial future.

FINANCING FUNDAMENTALS: EXPLORING YOUR **INVESTMENT OPTIONS**

Alright, my future real estate moguls, let's get down to brass tacks. You've set your goals, you've scoped out your market, and now it's time to talk about the thing that makes the real estate world go round: money. Specifically, other people's money. Because let's be real—if we all had a vault full of cash like Scrooge McDuck, we wouldn't need to worry about financing, right?

But since most of us aren't swimming in gold coins, we've got to get creative. Financing is where the rubber meets the road in real estate, and if you play your cards right, you can turn a little bit of cash into a whole lot of property. So grab your calculator, put on your banker's hat, and let's dive into the wonderful world of financing.

The Myth of the Cash Buyer

Before we get into the nitty-gritty, let's debunk a myth: you do NOT need to be a cash buyer to succeed in real estate. Sure, if you've got a few million lying around, you can skip this chapter and go straight to the closing table. But for the rest of us, financing is the key to unlocking those shiny front doors.

Think of financing as your best friend in real estate. It's like having a rich uncle who's willing to lend you money—as long as you promise to pay it back with a little interest on top. The trick is knowing which financing option is right for you and your investment strategy. And trust me, there are more options than you can shake a stick at.

Option 1: Traditional Mortgages—The Classic

Let's start with the granddaddy of them all: the traditional mortgage. This is your classic 15- or 30-year loan where you put down a percentage of the property's price (usually 20%, but we'll get to that) and the bank covers the rest. You pay them back in monthly installments, plus interest, and voila—you're a homeowner.

Traditional mortgages are great if you've got a decent credit score, a steady income, and you're looking to hold onto the property for a while. They're stable, predictable, and come with the added bonus of making you feel like a responsible adult.

Pros:

- **Low Interest Rates:** Traditional mortgages typically offer the lowest interest rates, especially if you have good credit.
- **Long-Term Stability:** With fixed monthly payments, you know exactly what you're in for.
- **Tax Benefits:** The interest you pay on your mortgage is often tax-deductible. Score!

Cons:

- **Down Payment:** You'll need to cough up 20% of the property's value for a conventional loan, and let's face it—20% of a lot of money is still a lot of money.

- **Qualifying:** Banks aren't exactly handing out mortgages like candy. You'll need a solid credit score, proof of income, and a good debt-to-income ratio.

Option 2: FHA Loans—The First-Time Buyer's Best Friend

If you're new to the game and don't have a giant pile of cash for a down payment, FHA loans are like the cool aunt who slips you $20 when your parents aren't looking. FHA (Federal Housing Administration) loans are designed for first-time buyers and people with lower credit scores. They require a lower down payment—sometimes as low as 3.5%—and are generally easier to qualify for.

Pros:

- **Low Down Payment:** Only 3.5% down means you can get into a property without draining your savings.
- **Easier Approval:** The credit score requirements are more relaxed compared to conventional loans.
- **Assumable Loans:** If you sell the property, the buyer can take over your FHA loan, which can make your property more attractive.

Cons:

- **Mortgage Insurance:** FHA loans come with mandatory mortgage insurance premiums, which can add to your monthly payments.
- **Property Standards:** The property has to meet certain standards to qualify for an FHA loan, which might limit your options.

Option 3: VA Loans—For the Heroes Among Us

If you've served in the military, first of all, thank you for your service. Secondly, you've earned yourself one of the best deals in real estate: the VA loan. VA loans are backed by the Department of Veterans Affairs and offer incredible benefits, like no down payment and no private mortgage insurance (PMI).

Pros:

- **No Down Payment:** Zero. Zilch. Nada. You can finance 100% of the purchase price.

- **No PMI:** Unlike FHA loans, VA loans don't require private mortgage insurance, saving you money every month.

- **Competitive Interest Rates:** VA loans often come with lower interest rates than conventional loans.

Cons:

- **Funding Fee:** While there's no PMI, there is a one-time funding fee, although it can be rolled into the loan.

- **Eligibility:** You need to be a veteran, active-duty service member, or eligible family member to qualify.

Option 4: Hard Money Loans—For the Risk-Taker

Now we're getting into the wild side of financing. Hard money loans are short-term, high-interest loans from private lenders, usually used for fix-and-flip projects or when you need money fast. They're based more on the property's value than your creditworthiness, which means they're great if you've got a less-than-stellar credit history but have found a killer deal.

Pros:

- **Fast Approval:** Hard money lenders can get you the cash in a matter of days, not weeks.

- **Flexible Terms:** These loans are more flexible in terms of repayment schedules and requirements.

- **Great for Flipping:** If you need quick cash to buy, renovate, and sell a property, hard money loans can be a lifesaver.

Cons:

- **High Interest Rates:** We're talking double digits here. Hard money doesn't come cheap.
- **Short-Term:** These loans are usually for 6-12 months, so you need to have an exit strategy in place.
- **Risk:** If you can't sell or refinance the property quickly, you could find yourself in hot water.

Option 5: Private Money—Your Network Is Your Net Worth

Private money is like borrowing from your Uncle Bob, but hopefully with a little more professionalism. These are loans from individuals—friends, family, or other investors—who are willing to finance your real estate deal. The terms are flexible and often based on your relationship with the lender.

Pros:

- **Flexibility:** Private lenders are often more flexible with terms, interest rates, and repayment schedules.
- **Creative Financing:** You can negotiate terms that work for both parties, including profit sharing arrangements.
- **Speed:** Like hard money, private loans can be funded quickly, making them great for time-sensitive deals.

Cons:

- **Relationship Risk:** Borrowing from friends or family can strain relationships if things go south.
- **Higher Interest Rates:** Depending on the lender, you might pay more than you would with a traditional mortgage.

- **Lack of Regulation:** Since these loans aren't regulated like traditional ones, you need to make sure everything is documented properly to avoid legal headaches.

Option 6: Seller Financing—Cutting Out the Middleman

Seller financing is like ordering directly from the chef instead of going through a waiter. In this scenario, the seller acts as the lender, and you make payments directly to them. It's a great option if the seller owns the property outright and is willing to finance the deal themselves.

Pros:

- **No Bank Involvement:** You don't have to deal with banks, which means less paperwork and faster closing.
- **Flexible Terms:** Since you're dealing directly with the seller, you can negotiate terms that work for both parties.
- **Easier Qualification:** If you've got credit issues, seller financing can be easier to qualify for than a traditional mortgage.

Cons:

- **Higher Interest Rates:** Sellers might charge higher interest rates than traditional lenders.
- **Balloon Payments:** Some seller financing deals include a balloon payment, where the remaining balance is due in full after a certain period.
- **Limited Availability:** Not all sellers are willing to finance a deal, so this option can be harder to find.

Choose Your Weapon Wisely

So there you have it—your guide to the wild world of real estate financing. Whether you're going the traditional route with a mortgage, getting creative with private money, or taking a walk on the wild side with hard money, the key is to find the financing option that best fits your strategy and your goals.

Remember, financing isn't just about getting the money you need; it's about getting it in a way that sets you up for success. So do your homework, compare your options, and choose wisely. After all, the right financing can turn a good deal into a great one—and make you feel like a real estate rockstar in the process.

Now go out there, secure that financing, and make some deals happen. Your future empire is waiting!

A Personal Story: Jey's Strategic Edge: How Smart Financing Turned a Property Investment into a Game-Changer

Let me share a story that perfectly illustrates the power of choosing the right financing option. Meet Jey, a young entrepreneur with a big dream. Jey was a tech-savvy professional with a knack for spotting trends and a passion for real estate. After a few years of hustling and saving, he was ready to dive into the property market. But here's the catch: Jey wasn't just looking for any investment. He wanted to make a splash with a property that would generate substantial passive income while also appreciating in value.

The challenge? Figuring out which financing option would give him the best chance to hit those goals. Jey had a few options on the table, and each came with its own set of advantages and hurdles. It was time to cut through the noise and find out what would work best for him.

Jey had his eye on a multi-family property in a burgeoning neighborhood. He'd done his homework—he knew the location was prime, the rent rolls were strong, and the property was poised for appreciation. But when it came to financing, things got a bit murky. Should he go for a traditional mortgage, a hard money loan, or perhaps leverage his existing home equity?

We sat down and mapped out his goals. Jey wanted to maximize his cash flow while keeping his monthly payments manageable. He didn't want to tie up too much of his own cash upfront, but he also wanted to avoid high-interest loans that could eat into his profits.

First on the list was the traditional mortgage. Jey could secure a fixed-rate mortgage with a solid down payment, which would provide stability and predictability. It was a safe bet, but it required a hefty 20% down and had a relatively long approval process. Not to mention, it might limit his ability to invest in additional properties right away.

Next, we looked at hard money loans. These loans would provide quick cash and were perfect for high-risk investments. But the trade-off? Sky-high interest rates and short terms. Hard money loans are great for flipping properties but less ideal for long-term holds. This wasn't quite what Jey needed for a steady rental income stream.

Then there was the option of tapping into his home equity. Jey had built significant equity in his current home, and a home equity line of credit (HELOC) could offer flexible, low-interest financing. This option allowed him to borrow against his existing property without disrupting his cash flow. It was a compelling choice, but he needed to weigh it against the other options.

After a thorough analysis, Jey decided to go with the home equity option. Why? It offered the best balance of low interest, flexibility, and accessibility. By leveraging his home equity, he could secure the funds he needed for the down payment and renovation costs without overextending himself financially. It allowed him to maintain his cash reserves while still pursuing his investment goals.

Jey moved forward with a HELOC, and the results were impressive. He secured the multi-family property, made some strategic upgrades, and soon had a steady stream of rental income. The property appreciated as expected, and Jey's careful financing decision paid off. His initial choice allowed him to maximize returns while keeping his investment strategy agile.

Jey's story is a perfect example of how the right financing can transform a potential investment into a thriving success. It's not just about picking a loan —it's about selecting a financing strategy that aligns with your goals and financial situation. By choosing the home equity option, Jey turned a great opportunity into a lucrative reality.

So, if you're in the market for real estate investment, remember Jey's journey. Evaluate your options, consider your goals, and choose the financing that sets you up for success. With the right strategy, you'll turn those real estate dreams into a powerful, profitable reality.

PART II
TAKING **ACTION**

BUILDING YOUR TEAM: ASSEMBLING THE RIGHT EXPERTS

Alright, future real estate tycoons, let's have a little chat about teamwork. I know, I know—when you think of real estate, you probably imagine yourself as a one-person powerhouse, wheeling and dealing, making all the big decisions, and rolling in the profits. And while it's true that you're the star of this show, even the biggest stars have an entourage. You don't see Beyoncé setting up her own stage, do you? Exactly.

Real estate isn't a solo sport—it's a team game. And if you want to win big, you need a dream team that's as dedicated to your success as you are. We're talking about assembling a crack squad of experts who will make sure you don't end up buying a money pit or signing a contract that gives you hives.

So, who do you need on your team? Let's break it down.

The Real Estate Agent: Your Right-Hand Man (or Woman)

First up, the real estate agent. This is the person who's going to be by your side through thick and thin, helping you navigate the choppy waters of the market. Think of them as your real estate therapist—they'll listen to your dreams, calm your fears, and gently steer you away from that "charming fixer-upper" that's more "horror movie set" than "dream home."

What to Look For:

- **Experience:** You want someone who's been around the block—literally. An agent with experience in your target market knows the neighborhoods, the trends, and the hidden gems.

- **Negotiation Skills:** Your agent should be able to negotiate like a pro. If they can't haggle down the price or get you the best terms, you might as well just hand over your wallet.

- **Compatibility:** You're going to spend a lot of time with this person, so make sure you like them. If they make you want to pull your hair out after five minutes, it's not going to work.

The Lender: Your Money Guy (or Gal)

Next up is the lender. This is the person who's going to make sure you have the cash to close the deal. Think of them as your financial fairy godmother, except instead of a pumpkin, they'll turn your pre-approval letter into a home loan.

What to Look For:

- **Competitive Rates:** Not all loans are created equal. You want a lender who can offer you the best interest rates and terms.

- **Transparency:** Your lender should be upfront about all the costs involved. If they're hiding fees or glossing over details, run.

- **Responsiveness:** Real estate moves fast, and you need a lender who's going to keep up. If they take days to return your calls, you might miss out on your dream deal.

The Real Estate Attorney: Your Legal Eagle

Now, let's talk lawyers. If contracts make your head spin, you need a real estate attorney. This person will make sure all the legal mumbo jumbo is in order and that you don't sign something that will come back to bite you later. Think of them as your personal bouncer—they're not letting anything sketchy get past the door.

What to Look For:

- **Specialization:** You want an attorney who specializes in real estate, not your cousin's friend who "dabbles" in everything from divorces to dog bites.

- **Attention to Detail:** Real estate contracts can be long and boring, but they're full of crucial details. Your attorney should have the patience of a saint and the eye of a hawk.

- **Problem-Solver:** Deals don't always go smoothly. You need an attorney who can think on their feet and find solutions when things go sideways.

The Inspector: The Eagle-Eyed Detective

You wouldn't buy a car without checking under the hood, right? The same goes for houses. That's where the inspector comes in. This person's job is to go over the property with a fine-tooth comb and find anything that could cause problems down the road. Leaky roof? Faulty wiring? Weird smells coming from the basement? Your inspector is on it.

What to Look For:

- **Experience:** The more houses they've inspected, the better. You want someone who's seen it all and knows what to look for.

- **Thoroughness:** Your inspector should leave no stone

unturned, no nook or cranny unchecked. If they're in and out in 20 minutes, that's a red flag.

- **Communication:** A good inspector doesn't just find problems—they explain them to you in a way you can understand. You don't need a technical manual, just clear, actionable information.

The Contractor: Your Fix-It Pro

If you're buying a fixer-upper, or just want to make some improvements, you'll need a contractor. This is the person who's going to turn your vision into reality—without running over budget or taking forever to finish. A good contractor is worth their weight in gold; a bad one will make you wish you'd never heard the words "home renovation."

What to Look For:

- **Reputation:** Ask around, read reviews, and check references. A good contractor has a solid reputation and a portfolio of completed projects to prove it.

- **Punctuality:** If they can't show up to meetings on time, how do you think the project will go? Punctuality is a good indicator of how seriously they take their work.

- **Problem-Solving:** Every renovation has its challenges. You want someone who can think on their feet and find solutions without freaking out (or charging you an arm and a leg).

The Property Manager: Your Time-Saving Hero

If you're investing in rental properties, a property manager is your best friend. They handle the day-to-day headaches so you don't have to—everything from finding tenants to fixing leaky faucets. Basically, they make your life easier while your investment works for you.

What to Look For:

- **Experience with Rentals:** Property management is a whole different ballgame. You want someone who knows how to handle tenants, maintenance issues, and the occasional 3 a.m. emergency call.

- **Organization:** A good property manager is on top of everything—rent payments, maintenance schedules, tenant issues. If they're organized, your property will be in good hands.

- **Communication:** You need someone who keeps you in the loop without bombarding you with every little detail. Clear, concise updates are the name of the game.

The Accountant: The Number Cruncher

Finally, we've got the accountant. This is the person who's going to make sure all the numbers add up and that Uncle Sam doesn't take more than his fair share. They'll help you with everything from tax deductions to bookkeeping, so you can focus on making deals instead of crunching numbers.

What to Look For:

- **Real Estate Experience:** Not all accountants are created equal. You want one who knows the ins and outs of real estate tax laws and can help you maximize your deductions.

- **Attention to Detail:** In accounting, the devil is in the details. A good accountant catches the little things that can make a big difference in your bottom line.

- **Proactive:** A great accountant doesn't just react—they plan ahead. They'll help you strategize for tax season and beyond, so there are no nasty surprises.

Assembling Your A-Team

So there you have it—the dream team you need to crush it in

real estate. Remember, you don't have to do it all yourself. The best real estate investors know how to delegate, and they surround themselves with experts who have their backs.

Assembling the right team isn't just about finding people who are good at what they do—it's about finding people who understand your goals, share your vision, and are just as committed to your success as you are.

So go out there, find your squad, and start making things happen. Because with the right team in your corner, there's no deal too big, no problem too tough, and no goal too ambitious. Let's go build something great.

A Personal Story: How Mark, a U.S. Navy Sailor, Built His Powerhouse Real Estate Team

Let me share the story of Mark, a dedicated U.S. Navy Sailor who turned his military discipline and strategic mindset into a winning formula for real estate success. Mark's journey from the deck of a Navy destroyer to the world of real estate investing is a testament to how applying military precision and teamwork can lead to extraordinary achievements.

The Mission: Building a Real Estate Portfolio

After years of serving in the Navy, Mark was ready for a new challenge. He had a clear mission: to build a portfolio of rental properties that would generate passive income and appreciate in value. Mark knew that just like a well-coordinated naval operation, he needed a stellar team to achieve his goals.

Finding the Real Estate Agent: The Market Navigator

Mark's first step was to find a real estate agent who could guide him through the complex waters of the property market. He needed someone who knew the local market inside out and could spot opportunities like a seasoned scout. Mark leveraged his network and sought advice from fellow veterans who had ventured into real estate. That's how he was introduced to Elena, a real estate agent with an impressive track record and deep market knowledge. Elena was known for her strategic approach and ability to identify high-potential properties.

From day one, Elena proved to be an invaluable ally. Her expertise helped Mark secure his first property in an up-and-coming neighborhood, setting the stage for his success. Elena's strategic insights were exactly what Mark needed to navigate the competitive real estate landscape.

Selecting the Real Estate Attorney: The Legal Expert

With Elena's help, Mark moved to the next phase: securing a real estate attorney. Mark knew the importance of having a legal expert who could handle the intricate details of property transactions and protect his interests. Mark reached out to his network and was referred to David, a real estate attorney known for his meticulous work and ability to handle complex legal issues. David's reputation for thoroughness and clear communication made him the ideal choice.

When Mark encountered a potential legal issue with a property title, David stepped in and resolved the matter efficiently. Thanks to David's expertise, Mark was able to proceed with his investment without any legal setbacks.

Partnering with the Lender: The Financial Strategist

Next, Mark needed a lender who could provide flexible financing solutions and help him navigate the world of mortgages. He wanted someone who could tailor financing to fit his investment strategy.

Mark found his financial strategist in Carla, a mortgage broker renowned for her innovative financing solutions. Carla's ability to understand Mark's needs and find the best loan products was crucial for his success.

When Mark decided to expand his portfolio with a larger multifamily property, Carla helped him secure a loan with favorable terms. Her financial expertise allowed Mark to maintain liquidity while investing in high-value assets.

Hiring the Property Inspector: The Property Sleuth

Mark knew that before closing any deal, a thorough property inspection was essential. He needed an inspector who could uncover hidden issues and provide a detailed assessment of each property.

Mark hired Laura, an inspector with a reputation for her keen eye and detailed reports. Laura's thorough inspections saved Mark from potential pitfalls and ensured that each property met his standards.

On one occasion, Laura discovered significant foundation issues in a property Mark was interested in. Her findings allowed Mark to renegotiate the deal and avoid a costly mistake.

Engaging the Property Manager: The Operational Specialist

As Mark's portfolio grew, he needed a property manager to handle the day-to-day operations of his rental properties. He wanted someone reliable who could ensure his properties were well-maintained and tenants were satisfied.

Mark found James, a property manager with a proven track record of excellence. James's proactive approach and attention to detail ensured that Mark's properties ran smoothly, and tenant issues were resolved efficiently. With James handling the operational aspects, Mark could focus on expanding his portfolio and pursuing new opportunities. James's expertise was crucial in maintaining the high standards Mark set for his properties.

Consulting the Accountant: The Financial Guru

The final piece of Mark's team was an accountant who could manage the financial aspects of his investments and provide strategic tax advice. Mark needed someone who understood the complexities of real estate finance.
Mark enlisted Sarah, a CPA with extensive experience in real estate. Sarah's insights into tax strategies and financial management helped Mark optimize his returns and manage his finances effectively.

Sarah's guidance was invaluable during tax season, helping Mark navigate deductions and credits. Her strategic advice also helped Mark plan for future investments and manage cash flow.

The Outcome: A Thriving Investment Portfolio

With his team in place, Mark's real estate investments began to thrive. Each expert played a critical role in his success, from finding and financing properties to managing operations and handling legal matters. The synergy between Mark and his team led to a flourishing portfolio and impressive growth.

Mark's journey from a U.S. Navy Sailor to a successful real estate investor is a powerful example of how discipline, teamwork, and strategic thinking can lead to extraordinary results. By carefully selecting and working with top professionals, Mark turned his real estate dreams into a successful reality.

So, if you're ready to embark on your own real estate journey, take a page from Mark's playbook. Build your powerhouse team, leverage their expertise, and watch your investment goals transform into a thriving success. With the right team by your side, the possibilities are limitless.

PROPERTY HUNT: FINDING THE PERFECT INVESTMENT **OPPORTUNITY**

Alright, real estate rockstars, it's time to roll up your sleeves and get to the heart of the action—the property hunt. This is where the rubber meets the road, the game gets real, and you start transforming those big dreams into concrete (or maybe brick, or wood, or steel—depends on the property, right?).

Finding the perfect investment opportunity is like dating: you're searching for "the one" that checks all your boxes, doesn't come with too much baggage, and will give you a good return on your emotional (and financial) investment. And just like dating, it can be exciting, frustrating, and downright confusing. But don't worry—I'm here to guide you through the process with a little humor and a lot of real estate know-how.

A. Know What You Want—Before You Start Swiping Right

First things first: you need to know what you're looking for before you start the search. Going into the property hunt without a clear idea of what you want is like going to the grocery store when you're starving—you're going to end up with a bunch of stuff you don't need and probably regret buying later.

So, let's get clear on your criteria:

- **Budget:** How much are you willing (and able) to spend? This isn't just about the purchase price—factor in closing costs, potential repairs, and a little cushion for unexpected surprises. If you spend all your cash on the property and forget about the rest, you'll be in for a rough ride.

- **Property Type:** Are you looking for a single-family home, a multi-family property, a condo, or something else? Each type of property comes with its own set of pros and cons. Single-family homes are easy to manage but might not offer as high a return as multi-family units. Condos have lower maintenance but come with HOA fees. Know what you're getting into.

- **Location, Location, Location:** You've heard this one a million times, but it's true—location is everything. Are you targeting an urban area, a suburb, or a rural location? What's the neighborhood like? Is it up-and-coming or on the decline? Remember, you can fix a house, but you can't fix a neighborhood.

- **Condition:** Are you up for a fixer-upper, or do you want something move-in ready? Fixer-uppers can be great if you're handy or have a good contractor, but they can also turn into a money pit if you're not careful. Move-in ready properties are easier but might come with a higher price tag.

- **Potential for Appreciation:** You're not just buying for today—you're buying for the future. Look for properties in areas where you expect values to rise. This might be due to planned developments, new businesses moving in, or a general trend of gentrification. You want to buy where the market is heading, not where it's been.

Location, Location, Location- The Unbreakable Rule of Real Estate:

If there's one rule in real estate that's as old as time itself, it's this: **location matters.** It's not just a cliché; it's the bedrock of real estate success. Whether you're investing in a single-family home, a skyscraper, or anything in between, where you buy can be just as important—if not more so—than what you buy. The right location can elevate an average property to a goldmine, while the wrong one can turn a great property into a financial drain. Let's break down why location is the foundation upon which every successful real estate investment is built.

Demand and Supply: The Core of Market Dynamics

Real estate is all about demand and supply, and location is the primary driver of both. High-demand areas attract more buyers and renters, leading to higher property values and rental rates. Conversely, low-demand areas struggle to attract interest, which can suppress prices and make properties harder to rent or sell.

Key Factors Influencing Demand:

- **Economic Growth:** Areas with strong economies, job opportunities, and growing industries attract more
- **Population Trends:** Urbanization, migration patterns, and demographic shifts all impact demand. Cities or regions experiencing population growth are likely to see increased demand for housing and commercial space.
- **Scarcity of Land:** In densely populated areas or cities with limited space for new development, the scarcity of land drives up property values. This is why real estate in major metropolitan areas tends to be more expensive.

Neighborhood Quality: The Power of Local Appeal

Within a broader location, the quality of the neighborhood plays a critical role in determining a property's value and attractiveness. The best properties are often found in neighborhoods that offer a combination of safety, amenities, and a sense of community.

Key Neighborhood Attributes:

- **Safety:** Low crime rates are a top priority for most homebuyers and renters. Properties in safe neighborhoods tend to have higher values and attract more interest.

- **Schools:** Proximity to high-quality schools is a major draw for families. Homes in top school districts often command premium prices and enjoy strong demand.

- **Amenities:** Access to amenities like parks, shopping centers, restaurants, and entertainment options makes a neighborhood more attractive. The convenience of nearby amenities can significantly enhance a property's value.

- **Community:** A strong sense of community, including active neighborhood associations and local events, can make an area more desirable and drive demand.

Proximity to Key Locations: Accessibility Drives Value

In real estate, being close to key locations—like business districts, transportation hubs, and cultural attractions—can significantly impact a property's value and rental potential. The easier it is for people to get to work, school, or entertainment, the more attractive a property becomes.

Key Considerations:

- **Workplaces:** Proximity to major employment centers or business districts is a huge draw, especially in urban areas. Properties near office complexes, industrial parks, or downtown areas tend to have higher demand and rents.

- **Transportation:** Access to public transportation, highways, and major roads increases a property's accessibility. Properties near metro stations, bus stops, or major highways are often more desirable, particularly in densely populated areas.

- **Cultural and Recreational Sites:** Being close to cultural attractions, historical landmarks, parks, and recreational facilities can boost a property's appeal. These locations enhance the quality of life for residents and can increase the desirability of nearby properties.

Future Development: The Value of Growth Potential

Investing in an area with strong future growth potential is like buying a stock before it skyrockets. Locations poised for development—whether through new infrastructure, commercial projects, or residential expansions—can offer significant appreciation opportunities.

Key Indicators of Future Growth:

- **Planned Infrastructure Projects:** New highways, bridges, public transit expansions, and airport improvements can make an area more accessible and attractive, driving up property values.

- **Commercial Development:** The arrival of new businesses, shopping centers, or entertainment districts can transform an area, increasing demand for nearby residential and commercial properties.

- **Urban Revitalization:** In cities, areas undergoing revitalization or gentrification often see a surge in property values. Investors who buy early in these neighborhoods can benefit from significant appreciation as the area improves.

- **Government Initiatives:** Local government plans for

development, such as tax incentives for businesses or housing developments, can indicate an area's growth potential.

Market Stability: The Safety Net of a Solid Location

A good location isn't just about growth—it's also about stability. In volatile markets, properties in prime locations tend to hold their value better than those in less desirable areas. A well-chosen location can serve as a safety net during economic downturns or market corrections.

Key Stability Indicators:

- **Historical Performance:** Look at the property values in the area over the past decade. Stable or steadily rising prices indicate a resilient market.

- **Diverse Economy:** Areas with a diverse economic base—multiple industries rather than reliance on a single sector—are less susceptible to economic downturns.

- **Strong Community Ties:** Neighborhoods with strong, established communities are less likely to see drastic declines in property values, even in tough times.

Local Market Conditions: The Micro-Market Advantage

Even within the same city, different neighborhoods or districts can perform very differently. Understanding the micro-market conditions—specific trends and characteristics of a small, localized area—can give you an edge in identifying lucrative opportunities.

Micro-Market Considerations:

- **Supply and Demand Dynamics:** Pay attention to the number of properties available for sale or rent in the area. A low supply of properties in a high-demand area is a good indicator of a strong market.

- **Local Regulations:** Zoning laws, property taxes, and other regulations can vary widely between areas. Understanding these factors can help you identify locations with favorable conditions for investment.

- **Neighborhood Life Cycle:** Is the neighborhood emerging, stabilizing, or declining? Investing in a neighborhood on the rise can yield significant returns, but be cautious of areas in decline without signs of revitalization.

The Location Formula for Success

Location is the ultimate determinant of a property's success. It's the factor that can elevate your investment from average to exceptional. By choosing a location with strong demand, quality neighborhoods, proximity to key sites, and growth potential, you set yourself up for long-term success. But remember, real estate is local, and every market is unique. Do your homework, trust your instincts, and always keep your finger on the pulse of the location. Because in real estate, the right location isn't just an advantage—it's everything.

Property Types:

When it comes to real estate, the type of property you choose is your first big decision. It's like picking the right vehicle for a road trip—you need the one that'll get you where you want to go, with the least bumps along the way. So, let's dive into the different property types and why each could be your golden ticket in this game.

Single-Family Homes: The Classic Starter

Single-family homes are the bread and butter of residential real estate. Think of them as the Swiss Army knife of properties—versatile, straightforward, and always in demand.

Whether you're flipping, renting, or holding, these properties offer a ton of flexibility.

Why They're a Win:

- **High Demand:** Everyone needs a place to live, and single-family homes are the most sought-after. They're the go-to for families, individuals, and even retirees looking for a slice of the American Dream.

- **Appreciation Potential:** These homes often appreciate steadily over time, especially in growing markets. It's a long-term play that pays off when you're ready to sell.

- **Easier Management:** Compared to multifamily or commercial properties, managing a single-family home is a walk in the park. Fewer tenants mean fewer headaches.

Multifamily Properties: Cash Flow Machines

Next up, we've got multifamily properties. Think of these as the muscle cars of real estate—built for power, speed, and serious cash flow. If your goal is to generate consistent income, multifamily units are where the money's at.

Why They're a Win:

- **Multiple Income Streams:** With more units under one roof, you're collecting rent from several tenants. That's multiple checks in your pocket every month.

- **Risk Mitigation:** Even if one unit is vacant, you've got others bringing in income. It's like having a safety net for your cash flow.

- **Economies of Scale:** Maintaining one building with multiple units is often more cost-effective than managing several single-family homes spread out across town.

Condominiums: The Low-Maintenance Play

Condos are like the luxury sedans of the real estate world—

sleek, low-maintenance, and often located in prime urban areas. If you're looking for an investment that's relatively hands-off, a condo might be your best bet.

Why They're a Win:

- **Prime Locations:** Condos are usually found in desirable urban locations where land is scarce and demand is high. That means higher rents and strong appreciation potential.

- **Minimal Maintenance:** With a condo, you're only responsible for the interior of your unit. The homeowners' association (HOA) handles the exterior, landscaping, and amenities.

- **Attractive to Renters:** Many renters, especially young professionals, are drawn to the convenience and amenities that condos offer, such as gyms, pools, and security.

Commercial Properties: The Power Play

Now, if you're looking to level up and play in the big leagues, commercial properties are your ticket. These are like the private jets of real estate—high stakes, high rewards, and not for the faint of heart.

Why They're a Win:

- **Long-Term Leases:** Commercial tenants often sign multi-year leases, providing stable, predictable income for the long haul.

- **High Returns:** Commercial properties generally offer higher returns than residential properties, especially in prime business districts.

- **Triple Net Leases (NNN):** In some commercial deals, tenants cover property taxes, insurance, and maintenance, reducing your operational costs and boosting your net income.

Vacation Rentals: The Cash-Flowing Getaway

Vacation rentals are like the luxury sports cars of real estate—flashy, exciting, and capable of generating serious revenue when done right. With the rise of platforms like Airbnb and VRBO, short-term rentals are a hot market.

Why They're a Win:

- **High Income Potential:** Vacation rentals can generate significantly higher income than traditional long-term rentals, especially in popular tourist destinations.

- **Flexibility:** You can rent them out when demand is high and even enjoy them yourself during the off-season.

- **Appreciation in Hot Markets:** Properties in desirable vacation spots often appreciate faster, adding value to your investment over time.

Industrial Properties: The Steady Workhorse

Industrial properties might not be as glamorous, but they're the workhorses of real estate. Think of them as the heavy-duty trucks—built to last, reliable, and essential to the economy.

Why They're a Win:

- **Stable Tenants:** Industrial tenants, like manufacturing companies or warehouses, tend to stay for long periods, providing steady income.

- **Low Maintenance:** These properties usually require less upkeep compared to residential or commercial properties, which means lower costs.

- **Growth Sector:** With the rise of e-commerce, the demand for industrial space—like distribution centers—is booming, making this a growing market.

Mixed-Use Properties: The Best of Both Worlds

Mixed-use properties are the hybrids of real estate, combining residential, commercial, and sometimes even industrial spaces. They're like a tricked-out SUV—versatile, practical, and capable of handling multiple terrains.

Why They're a Win:

- **Diversified Income Streams:** With multiple types of tenants, you're not putting all your eggs in one basket. You've got residential rent, commercial lease payments, and maybe even some retail income.

- **Prime Locations:** Mixed-use properties are often located in vibrant, walkable neighborhoods, attracting both residents and businesses.

- **Community Appeal:** These properties create a sense of community, offering everything from living spaces to shops and restaurants, all in one place.

Picking Your Ride

In real estate, the property type you choose sets the tone for your investment journey. Whether you're going for the steady cash flow of multifamily units, the low-maintenance allure of condos, or the high-stakes game of commercial properties, each option comes with its own set of rewards. The key is aligning your choice with your goals, risk tolerance, and market understanding. So, pick your ride, buckle up, and get ready to accelerate toward your real estate dreams.

The Investment Strategy Game:

When it comes to real estate investing, there's no one-size-fits-all approach. Each investor has unique goals, risk tolerance, and resources, which means your investment strategy should be tailored to what you want to achieve. Whether you're looking for steady cash flow, long-term appreciation, or a blend of both, understanding the different strategies available is key to making informed decisions. Let's break down some of the most effective real estate investment strategies that can help you build and grow your portfolio.

Buy and Hold: The Long Game

The buy-and-hold strategy is the classic approach where you purchase a property and hold onto it for an extended period, typically to benefit from both rental income and property appreciation over time. This strategy is about playing the long game and letting time work in your favor.

Benefits:

- **Steady Cash Flow:** By renting out the property, you generate consistent monthly income.
- **Appreciation:** Over time, the property is likely to increase in value, boosting your equity.
- **Tax Advantages:** Depreciation and other tax deductions can improve your overall return.
- **Leverage:** With a mortgage, you can control a valuable asset with a relatively small down payment.

Ideal For:
- Investors seeking long-term wealth accumulation.
- Those looking for a relatively passive income stream.
- Investors with patience and a long-term outlook.

House Flipping: The Quick Turnaround

House flipping involves buying a property, making improvements or renovations, and then selling it for a profit. This strategy is all about speed—getting in, adding value, and getting out with a solid return.

Benefits:

- **High Potential Profit:** If done correctly, flipping can yield substantial profits in a short amount of time.

- **Market Timing:** You can take advantage of hot markets and rising property values.

- **Personal Satisfaction:** Many investors enjoy the process of renovating and transforming a property.

Ideal For:
- Investors who are knowledgeable about the local market.
- Those with experience in construction or renovation.
- Investors willing to take on higher risk for the potential of higher rewards.

BRRRR Strategy: Buy, Rehab, Rent, Refinance, Repeat

The BRRRR strategy is a combination of buy-and-hold and flipping. You buy a distressed property, rehab it, rent it out to generate income, refinance to pull out your capital, and then repeat the process with another property. It's a cyclical strategy that allows you to build a portfolio with minimal upfront capital.

Benefits:

- **Equity Growth:** By rehabbing and renting, you build equity quickly.

- **Recycling Capital:** Refinancing lets you pull out your initial investment to fund the next deal.

- **Scalability:** This strategy allows for rapid portfolio growth without constantly needing new capital.

Ideal For:
- Investors with renovation experience.
- Those looking to build a large portfolio with minimal upfront capital.
- Investors who want to maximize returns by leveraging each property.

Short-Term Rentals: The Vacation Rental Play

Short-term rentals, like those listed on Airbnb or VRBO, involve renting out a property for short periods, usually to vacationers or business travelers. This strategy takes advantage of high nightly rates, especially in desirable locations.

Benefits:

- **Higher Income Potential:** Short-term rentals can generate higher monthly income compared to long-term rentals.
- **Flexibility:** You can adjust your rental rates based on demand and seasons.
- **Personal Use:** You can block off time for personal use of the property when it's not rented.

Ideal For:

- Investors in tourist-heavy areas or popular urban destinations.
- Those who can manage the higher turnover and guest interaction.
- Investors seeking a mix of personal enjoyment and income generation.

Wholesaling: The Quick Flip Without the Fix

Wholesaling involves finding a property, getting it under contract, and then selling that contract to another investor for a fee. You don't actually purchase the property yourself; instead, you act as the middleman between the seller and the end buyer.

Benefits:

- **Low Capital Requirement:** You don't need much money to start since you're not buying the property.

- **Quick Profits:** Wholesaling deals can close quickly, providing fast returns.
- **No Renovation Required:** Unlike flipping, you're not responsible for repairs or improvements.

Ideal For:

- Investors with strong negotiation skills and market knowledge.
- Those looking to generate income without owning property.
- New investors seeking to build capital before moving into other strategies.

Real Estate Investment Trusts (REITs): The Stock Market of Real Estate

REITs allow you to invest in real estate without actually owning physical properties. By purchasing shares in a REIT, you're investing in a portfolio of properties managed by a professional team, and you earn dividends based on the income generated by those properties.

Benefits:

- **Liquidity:** REITs are traded on stock exchanges, so you can buy and sell shares easily.
- **Diversification:** You gain exposure to a broad range of properties, reducing risk.
- **Passive Income:** REITs typically pay regular dividends, providing a steady income stream.

Ideal For:

- Investors looking for exposure to real estate without the hassles of property management.
- Those seeking a more liquid investment.
- Investors wanting to diversify their portfolio.

Buy, Rehab, Rent: The Long-Term Flipping Alternative

This strategy involves buying a property in need of renovation, rehabbing it, and then renting it out for long-term cash flow. It's a hybrid between flipping and buy-and-hold, where the rehab adds value and the rental income provides ongoing returns.

Benefits:

- **Increased Equity:** Renovating the property increases its value, boosting your equity.
- **Cash Flow:** Renting the property provides consistent income.
- **Tax Advantages:** You can take advantage of tax deductions related to both the rehab and the rental.

Ideal For:

- Investors who want to combine value-add with long-term income.
- Those with the patience to manage a renovation project.
- Investors looking for both cash flow and appreciation.

Commercial Real Estate: The Big Leagues

Investing in commercial real estate—such as office buildings, retail centers, or industrial properties—is a strategy that typically involves higher stakes but also higher rewards. Commercial properties are leased to businesses, often under long-term contracts.

Benefits:

- **Higher Returns:** Commercial properties generally offer higher returns than residential properties.
- **Long-Term Leases:** Businesses often sign leases for 5-10 years, providing stable, predictable income.

- **Professional Tenants:** Dealing with businesses can be less personal and more professional compared to residential tenants.

Ideal For:

- Experienced investors looking to diversify into larger, more complex deals.
- Those with a higher risk tolerance.
- Investors seeking long-term, stable cash flow.

Land Banking: Investing in the Future

Land banking involves buying undeveloped land in areas that are expected to grow in the future. The strategy is to hold the land until its value appreciates, then sell it for a profit or develop it yourself.

Benefits:

- **Potential for High Appreciation:** As the surrounding area develops, the value of the land can increase significantly.
- **Low Holding Costs:** Compared to developed properties, land has minimal maintenance costs.
- **Development Opportunities:** You can choose to develop the land yourself, increasing its value further.

Ideal For:

- Investors with a long-term horizon.
- Those who believe in the growth potential of a specific area.
- Investors willing to wait for the right time to sell.

Choosing the Right Strategy

The right real estate investment strategy depends on your goals, resources, and market conditions. Whether you're looking for quick flips, steady income, or long-term growth, there's a strategy out there that can help you achieve your objectives. The key is to do your homework, understand the risks and rewards, and be prepared to adapt as the market evolves. With the right strategy in place, you're well on your way to building a successful real estate portfolio.

B. The Tools of the Trade—Your Property Hunting Arsenal

Now that you know what you're looking for, it's time to arm yourself with the tools of the trade. The days of driving around neighborhoods with a notepad and a dream are over (unless you're into that kind of thing). Today, you've got a ton of resources at your disposal to make the hunt easier, faster, and a lot more fun.

Online Listings: Zillow, Realtor.com, Redfin—these are your new best friends. They're like Tinder for real estate, but with less awkward small talk. You can filter by price, location, property type, and more. Just remember, what you see online might not always match reality (thanks, Photoshop).

Real Estate Agents: A good agent is worth their weight in gold. They've got access to listings you might not see online, and they know the market inside and out. Plus, they can set up showings, negotiate deals, and guide you through the whole process. Think of them as your real estate wingman (or wingwoman).

Property Auctions: If you're feeling adventurous, property auctions can be a great way to snag a deal. Just make sure you do your homework—auctions move fast, and you don't want to get caught up in the heat of the moment and overpay. It's like eBay but with way bigger consequences.

Networking: Sometimes the best deals aren't listed anywhere—they come through word of mouth. Talk to other investors, real estate professionals, and even friends and family. You never know when a hot tip might come your way.

Driving for Dollars: Okay, I know I just said the days of driving around neighborhoods were over, but sometimes it's worth getting out there and seeing properties in person. You might spot a "For Sale by Owner" sign or a house that looks like it's ready for a new owner. Plus, you get a feel for the neighborhood that you can't get online.

C. Property Analysis: The Numbers Don't Lie

When you find a property that piques your interest, it's time to dive into the numbers. This is where you separate the promising opportunities from the duds. A thorough property analysis will give you a clear picture of the potential returns and risks associated with the investment.

Key metrics to analyze:

- **Cash Flow:** Calculate the expected cash flow by subtracting all expenses (mortgage, taxes, insurance, maintenance) from the rental income. Positive cash flow is a must for any rental property.

- **Cap Rate:** The capitalization rate (cap rate) measures the property's rate of return. It's calculated by dividing the net operating income (NOI) by the property's purchase price. A higher cap rate indicates a better return on investment.

- **ROI:** Return on investment (ROI) considers both cash flow and appreciation. It's a comprehensive measure of how well the property will perform over time.

- **Comparable Sales:** Look at similar properties in the area that have recently sold. This will give you an idea of the property's market value and potential appreciation.

Use these metrics to assess whether the property meets your investment goals. If the numbers don't add up, it's time to move on and continue the hunt.

D. Due Diligence: Uncover the Hidden Details

Even if a property looks perfect on paper, it's essential to conduct due diligence to uncover any hidden issues that could affect your investment. This is where you dig deeper into the property's condition, legal status, and any potential liabilities.

Key areas of due diligence:

- **Property Inspection:** Hire a professional inspector to evaluate the property's condition. Look for structural issues, outdated systems, and any repairs that could impact your budget.

- **Title Search:** Ensure the property has a clear title with no outstanding liens or legal disputes.

- **Zoning and Permits:** Verify that the property is zoned for your intended use and that all necessary permits are in place.

- **Environmental Concerns:** Check for any environmental issues, such as flood zones or contamination, that could affect the property's value or usability.

Due diligence is your last line of defense before committing to a purchase. Don't skip this step, as it could save you from costly surprises down the road.

E. Negotiation: Sealing the Deal

Once you've found the right property and completed your due

diligence, it's time to negotiate the deal. This is where your skills as a real estate investor come into play. Your goal is to secure the property at a price that maximizes your potential returns.

Key negotiation strategies:

- **Know the Market:** Use your market research to justify your offer. If the property is overpriced, present comparable sales to support your case.

- **Be Ready to Walk Away:** Don't get emotionally attached to the property. If the seller isn't willing to negotiate, be prepared to walk away. There are always other opportunities.

- **Leverage Inspection Results:** If the inspection uncovered issues, use them as leverage to negotiate a lower price or request repairs.

- **Offer Terms:** Sometimes, offering favorable terms, such as a quick closing or flexible payment options, can make your offer more attractive to the seller.

With a successful negotiation, you're ready to move forward and make the property yours.

F. Closing the Deal: Making It Official

The final step in the property hunt is closing the deal. This is where all your hard work comes together, and the property officially becomes yours. The closing process involves signing the necessary documents, transferring funds, and recording the deed.

Work closely with your attorney and lender to ensure a smooth closing process. Double-check all documents for accuracy and make sure you understand the terms of the purchase agreement. Once everything is in order, sign on the dotted line and celebrate your new investment.

The Hunt is On

Finding the perfect investment property is part science, part art, and a whole lot of fun. It's the thrill of the hunt that keeps us real estate junkies coming back for more. Sure, there are challenges, but with the right approach, a little patience, and a solid team behind you, you can find the property that's going to take you one step closer to your real estate dreams.

So get out there, start hunting, and remember: the perfect property is out there waiting for you. You just have to find it —and when you do, it's going to be epic. Happy hunting!

A Personal Story: How this U.S. Navy Sailor Set Himself Up For Life

Let me tell you about another client of mine, Chris, a U.S. Navy sailor with a strong desire to dive into real estate investing. Chris wasn't just looking for any property; he wanted the perfect investment—a property that would not only provide solid returns but also fit into his long-term plan for financial freedom.

When Chris first came to me, he was stationed in Norfolk, Virginia, and had saved up a decent amount from his deployments. He was eager to get started but didn't know exactly where to begin. Chris was laser-focused on finding a property that would set the foundation for his future portfolio, so we knew this had to be a strategic move.

We started by discussing his goals. Chris wanted a property that would generate cash flow while he was still on active duty, but he also wanted something that would appreciate over time—essentially, he was looking for the best of both worlds. He had a vision of eventually retiring from the Navy and transitioning into full-time real estate investing, so this first property was crucial.

The journey began with research. Lots of research. We dove into the local market, analyzing different neighborhoods in Hampton Roads. I showed Chris properties ranging from single-family homes to multifamily units, each with its pros and cons. But nothing clicked until we found a small multifamily property in an up-and-coming neighborhood just outside downtown Norfolk.

The property was a duplex, close to the naval base, which meant a steady stream of potential tenants—mostly military personnel like Chris. It was a bit of a fixer-upper, but that's where the opportunity lay. The location was prime: near public transportation, close to shops and restaurants, and in a neighborhood that was slowly but surely experiencing revitalization.

Chris could see the potential right away. The property had good bones, and with a bit of renovation, it could not only generate solid rental income but also appreciate significantly over the next few years. Plus, with the VA loan benefits, he could secure the property with minimal upfront cost, leaving him with more capital to invest in the renovations.

But the hunt wasn't over yet. We faced competition—other investors saw the same potential we did. It came down to making a strong, compelling offer that stood out. We crafted an offer that wasn't just about the price but also included a flexible closing date, understanding the seller's situation, and even a personal note from Chris, explaining how he planned to live in one unit while renting out the other, maintaining and improving the property over time.

The seller resonated with Chris's story, and we got the property under contract.

After closing, Chris rolled up his sleeves and got to work on the renovations. It wasn't easy, balancing his Navy duties with managing the renovation, but Chris was committed. He had a clear vision and was determined to bring it to life. In a few months, the property was transformed, and he quickly found tenants for the second unit.

Today, Chris's duplex is not just an investment; it's the cornerstone of his future real estate portfolio. The rental income covers the mortgage and then some, and the property's value has already started to increase as the neighborhood continues to develop. Chris is now planning his next move—possibly acquiring another property in the area—and he's on his way to achieving his goal of financial independence.

This journey taught Chris, and reminded me, that the perfect investment isn't just about the numbers; it's about aligning the property with your long-term goals, understanding the market, and being willing to put in the work to make it happen. Chris's story is a testament to what's possible when you approach real estate with strategy, patience, and a clear vision for the future.

CRUNCHING THE NUMBERS: ANALYZING POTENTIAL DEALS

When it comes to real estate investing, emotions can be your worst enemy. The excitement of finding a beautiful property or the allure of a "deal" can cloud your judgment and lead you down a path of financial regret. That's why, before you fall in love with any property, you need to put on your analytical hat and get down to the cold, hard numbers. This chapter is all about the art and science of analyzing potential deals—because in real estate, the numbers never lie.

Understanding the Basics: The Metrics That Matter

Before we dive into the specifics, let's start with the key metrics you need to understand. These are the financial indicators that will tell you whether a deal is worth pursuing or if you should walk away.

- **Cash Flow:** This is the net income you earn from a property after all expenses are paid. Positive cash flow means your property is generating more income than it's costing you, while negative cash flow means you're losing money each month.

- **Cap Rate (Capitalization Rate):** The cap rate is a measure of the property's return on investment, expressed as a percentage. It's calculated by dividing the property's net operating income (NOI) by its purchase price. A higher cap rate indicates a better return, but it also typically comes with higher risk.

- **Gross Rent Multiplier (GRM):** GRM is a simple way to evaluate the potential value of a property based on its gross rental income. It's calculated by dividing the property's purchase price by its annual rental income. While it's a useful quick check, it doesn't account for expenses, so it should be used alongside other metrics.

- **Return on Investment (ROI):** ROI measures the return you're getting on the money you've invested in the property. It's calculated by dividing the annual profit (or loss) by the total investment cost. This metric helps you compare the profitability of different investments.

- **Debt Service Coverage Ratio (DSCR):** DSCR is a measure of the property's ability to cover its debt obligations. It's calculated by dividing the NOI by the total debt service (the mortgage payments). A DSCR greater than 1 indicates that the property generates enough income to cover its debt, while a DSCR below 1 suggests the opposite.

The Power of Pro Formas: Projecting Future Performance

Once you understand the basic metrics, the next step is to project the property's financial performance over time. This is where a pro forma comes into play. A pro forma is a detailed financial model that estimates the income, expenses, and potential profit of a property over a specific period—typically five to ten years.

To create a pro forma, you'll need to gather the following information:

- **Projected Rental Income:** Start with the current rent rolls, but also consider market trends. Will you be able to raise rents in the future? How much vacancy should you expect?
- **Operating Expenses:** Include all costs associated with managing the property, such as property taxes, insurance, maintenance, property management fees, and utilities. Don't forget to budget for unexpected repairs and capital expenditures.
- **Financing Costs:** Include your mortgage payments, interest rates, and any other financing-related expenses.
- **Appreciation:** Estimate how much the property's value might increase over time. This is more art than science, but you can base your projections on historical appreciation rates in the area.

Once you have all this data, you can project the property's NOI, cash flow, and ROI over the investment period. A well-constructed pro forma will give you a clear picture of whether the property is likely to meet your investment goals.

Running the Scenarios: Stress Testing Your Deal

Real estate markets are dynamic, and things don't always go according to plan. That's why it's crucial to stress-test your pro forma by running different scenarios. Consider the following:

- What if the market softens and you can't raise rents as planned?
- What if the vacancy rate increases due to economic downturns?
- What if unexpected expenses arise?

By adjusting your assumptions and running worst-case, best-case, and most likely scenarios, you'll get a better sense of the risks involved. If your deal still looks solid even in the worst-case scenario, you're on the right track. If it falls apart, you might need to reconsider or negotiate better terms.

The 1% Rule: A Quick Screening Tool

If you're evaluating multiple properties, you need a quick way to screen out deals that don't meet your criteria. The 1% rule is a simple guideline that many investors use. According to the 1% rule, the monthly rental income should be at least 1% of the property's purchase price. For example, if you're looking at a $200,000 property, the monthly rent should be at least $2,000.

While the 1% rule is not a definitive measure of a good deal, it's a useful tool for quickly assessing whether a property is worth further analysis. If a property doesn't meet the 1% rule, it might still be a good investment, but you'll need to dig deeper into the numbers to find out why.

Leveraging Technology: Tools and Resources

Thanks to technology, analyzing deals has never been easier. There are countless apps, software, and online calculators that can help you crunch the numbers with precision. Some popular tools include:

- **Property Evaluator:** A mobile app that helps you analyze rental properties and flip deals with customizable pro formas and detailed reports.

- **DealCheck:** A web-based platform that allows you to analyze rental properties, BRRRR deals, flips, and multifamily investments. It also includes market data and rent estimates.

- **BiggerPockets Calculators:** A suite of online calculators for rental properties, flips, BRRRR deals, and more. These tools are especially useful for new investors.

By using these tools, you can streamline your analysis process, ensure accuracy, and make data-driven decisions.

Trusting Your Gut: When the Numbers Aren't Enough

While numbers are essential, they're not the whole story. Real estate investing is as much about intuition and experience as it is about math. Sometimes, a deal may look great on paper, but something feels off. Maybe it's the neighborhood, the condition of the property, or even the seller's behavior.

In these situations, it's important to trust your instincts. If something doesn't feel right, take a step back and reassess. It's better to miss out on a deal than to dive into something that could turn into a financial headache.

Knowing When to Walk Away

One of the hardest lessons for any real estate investor is knowing when to walk away. It's easy to get emotionally attached to a deal, especially after spending time analyzing and negotiating. But if the numbers don't add up, or if the risks outweigh the potential rewards, it's better to walk away and live to invest another day.

Remember, real estate investing is a marathon, not a sprint. There will always be more deals, and the right one will come along if you're patient and disciplined.

The Path to Financial Success

Analyzing potential deals is where the rubber meets the road in real estate investing. It's the difference between a successful investment and a financial disaster. By understanding the key metrics, creating detailed pro formas, stress-testing your assumptions, and trusting your instincts, you can make informed decisions that lead to long-term success.

The more you practice and refine your analysis skills, the better you'll become at identifying deals that align with your goals. So, get out there, crunch those numbers, and take the first step toward building your real estate empire.

The Calculated Leap: Alex's Journey from First-Time Investor to Real Estate Success

Let me tell you about one of my clients, a first-time investor who was eager to dive into real estate. Let's call him Alex. Alex was passionate about building wealth through real estate and had been saving diligently for this opportunity. His goal was to find a property that would not only generate steady rental income but also appreciate over time.

When Alex first reached out, he was excited but needed guidance on how to analyze potential deals. We began by evaluating various neighborhoods in Norfolk, Virginia, and soon came across a promising multifamily property—a four-unit building in a neighborhood showing signs of revitalization.

Alex was enthusiastic but knew he needed to assess the numbers carefully. We worked together to create a comprehensive pro forma, which included projected rental income, operating expenses, and financing costs. This pro forma was crucial for understanding the potential return on investment.

The property had potential, but it also needed some renovations. We factored these costs into our analysis and projected how much rent Alex could charge after the updates. We also considered potential vacancy rates and future interest rate fluctuations.

To make an informed decision, Alex ran multiple scenarios. The worst-case scenario showed that while the cash flow would be tight if unexpected issues arose, it would still be manageable. The best-case scenario projected a strong return on investment and significant appreciation. The most likely scenario indicated a steady, positive cash flow with room for growth.

With a solid understanding of the numbers, Alex decided to move forward. He made a competitive offer, negotiated the terms, and successfully acquired the property. During the renovation phase, Alex was hands-on, ensuring that everything was on track and within budget.

A few months after the renovations, the property was fully leased and generating the expected rental income. Not only did Alex achieve his goal of positive cash flow, but the property also began to appreciate in value, aligning perfectly with his long-term investment strategy.

Alex's journey highlights the importance of thorough financial analysis and strategic planning in real estate investing. By carefully crunching the numbers and preparing for different scenarios, he made a well-informed decision that set him up for future success in the real estate market.

THE ART OF NEGOTIATION: SECURING **THE BEST DEAL**

Alright, real estate warriors, you've done the hard work—you've set your goals, found the perfect market, assembled your dream team, and hunted down that perfect property. But before you pop the champagne and start planning your victory lap, there's one last hurdle to clear: negotiation.

Think of negotiation as the final showdown in an action movie. You're the hero, the seller is the worthy adversary, and the prize is that sweet, sweet property. This is where deals are won or lost, fortunes are made or missed, and reputations are either bolstered or busted. No pressure, right?

But don't worry—I've got your back. With the right mindset, a few tricks up your sleeve, and a dash of humor, you can walk away with a deal that would make even Gordon Gekko jealous. So, let's strap on our metaphorical boxing gloves and dive into the art of negotiation.

Know Your Worth—And Your Limits

First things first: before you even think about making an offer, you need to know your worth. This isn't just about your budget—it's about understanding the value of the property, the strength of your position, and what you're willing to compromise on.

Set Your Ceiling: Decide on the absolute maximum you're willing to pay for the property. This is your walk-away number—the point at which you shake hands, smile politely, and say, "Thanks, but no thanks." Knowing your ceiling ahead of time keeps you from getting caught up in the heat of the moment and overpaying.

Know the Property's Value: Do your homework. Look at comparable sales (comps), check out market trends, and understand the property's potential for appreciation. If you know the property's true value, you'll be in a much stronger position to negotiate.

Understand the Seller's Motivation: Are they eager to sell quickly, or are they holding out for top dollar? The more you know about the seller's situation, the better you can tailor your offer to their needs. If you know they're moving to Florida next week and need to close fast, you've got leverage.

Prioritize Your Must-Haves: Not every deal is going to give you everything you want. Identify your non-negotiables—whether it's the price, closing date, or certain repairs—and be prepared to compromise on the rest.

The Opening Offer: Make Your Move

The opening offer is like the first move in a game of chess. You want to come out strong, but not so strong that you scare off your opponent. It's about finding the right balance between assertiveness and flexibility.

Be Confident, Not Cocky: Confidence is key in negotiation. If you come in with a strong, well-reasoned offer, the seller is more likely to take you seriously. But don't be cocky—no one likes a know-it-all, and you don't want to start the negotiation off on the wrong foot.

Start Below Your Ceiling: This might seem obvious, but you'd be surprised how many people forget it in the heat of the moment. Always start your offer below your maximum budget. This gives you room to negotiate and makes it more likely you'll end up with a price you're happy with.

Justify Your Offer: Don't just throw out a number—back it up with facts. Use comps, market data, and the property's condition to justify your offer. If the roof needs replacing, mention it. If similar properties have sold for less, bring it up. The more logical your offer, the harder it is for the seller to dismiss it.

Show Willingness to Close Quickly: If you're in a position to close fast, use that to your advantage. Sellers often appreciate a quick, hassle-free sale, and they might be willing to drop the price a bit if you can get the deal done quickly.

The Counteroffer: Dance, Don't Duel

Negotiation isn't a duel to the death—it's a dance. The seller is going to counter, and when they do, it's your job to respond with grace, poise, and a little bit of strategy.

Don't Take It Personally: The seller's counteroffer isn't a personal attack—it's just business. Stay calm, stay focused, and keep your eye on the prize. Remember, they want to sell as much as you want to buy.

Counter with Care: When you counter their counter, don't just react—think strategically. This is where you might start making concessions on things that aren't deal-breakers for you. For example, if they won't budge on price, maybe you ask them to cover closing costs instead.

Use Silence as a Weapon: Sometimes the best move is no move at all. If the seller throws out a counteroffer and you don't respond right away, it can make them nervous. Silence can be a powerful tool in negotiation—it gives the impression that you're considering walking away, which might make the seller reconsider their position.

Be Ready to Walk: Speaking of walking away, don't be afraid to do it if the deal isn't right. Sometimes, the best way to secure a good deal is to be willing to walk away from a bad one. If the seller knows you're serious about walking, they might come back with a better offer.

The Power of Concessions: Give a Little, Get a Lot

Negotiation is all about give and take. The key is to give just enough to get what you really want. Think of it as a strategic game of "I'll scratch your back if you scratch mine."

Offer Non-Monetary Concessions: Not every concession has to be about money. Maybe you're willing to let the seller stay in the house a little longer after closing, or maybe you'll take care of a minor repair they're worried about. These kinds of concessions can be powerful bargaining chips.

Ask for Something in Return: If you give up something, ask for something in return. This keeps the negotiation balanced and shows that you're not just giving in—you're making a strategic trade.

Stay Flexible: Flexibility is your friend in negotiation. If the seller sees that you're willing to work with them, they're more likely to reciprocate. Just remember to keep your priorities straight—don't be so flexible that you bend over backwards and end up with a deal that doesn't make sense.

Closing the Deal: Victory Lap Time

You've danced the dance, made your moves, and now it's time to close the deal. This is the moment you've been waiting for—the point where all your hard work pays off.

Review Everything: Before you sign on the dotted line, review the contract carefully. Make sure all the terms you negotiated are in there, and double-check the numbers. This is where your attorney earns their keep—don't skip this step.

Stay Calm: Closing a deal can be nerve-wracking, especially if it's your first one. But stay calm, stay focused, and remember why you're doing this. You've negotiated a great deal, and now it's time to make it official.

Celebrate Smart: Once the deal is done, celebrate! But don't go too crazy—remember, you're a real estate investor now. Maybe a nice dinner or a bottle of champagne, but save the yacht parties for when you've closed a few more deals.

The Art of the Deal

Negotiation is where real estate investors separate the pros from the amateurs. It's a skill that takes time to master, but with practice, patience, and a little bit of strategy, you can secure deals that make your bank account sing.

Remember, negotiation isn't about winning or losing—it's about finding a deal that works for both parties. When done right, everyone walks away happy. So, go out there, sharpen your skills, and start making deals that would make even the shrewdest investors proud.

Because in real estate, the best deal isn't just the one that gets done—it's the one that gets done right.

Now go get 'em, champ!

Jordan Shoots the Game Winning Shot in Real Estate

Let me share the story of one of my clients, Jordan, who demonstrated exceptional skill in negotiating his first real estate deal.

Jordan had been eyeing the Norfolk market for a while. He was looking for his first investment property and had a clear vision: a multifamily unit that would provide steady cash flow and room for growth. After months of researching, Jordan found a promising four-unit building in a neighborhood on the verge of revitalization. The property was listed at a price slightly above his budget, but Jordan saw its potential.

Jordan approached the negotiation process with a strategic mindset. Here's how he navigated the art of negotiation to secure a deal that exceeded his expectations:

Preparation: Gathering Intelligence

Jordan knew that preparation was crucial. He started by conducting thorough market research. He analyzed recent sales of comparable properties in the area and discovered that the listing price of the building was on the higher end of the spectrum. This research armed him with the knowledge he needed to make a compelling case.

He also arranged for a detailed property inspection. The inspection revealed that while the building had great bones, it needed some significant repairs, including updates to plumbing and electrical systems. Jordan used these findings to inform his negotiation strategy.

Building Rapport: Connecting with the Seller

Jordan's first step was to build a connection with the seller. He made an effort to understand their situation, learning that the seller was relocating to another state and was eager to close the deal quickly. Jordan used this information to his advantage.

During his initial meeting with the seller, Jordan engaged in friendly conversation and showed genuine interest in the property's history and the seller's motivations. This rapport helped establish a positive and cooperative tone for the negotiations.

Making the Offer: Crafting a Strategic Proposal

Jordan made his offer based on his research and the property's inspection report. He started with a lower offer than the listing price, considering the needed repairs and the market data. However, his offer was well-supported by comparable sales and the inspection findings, which made it reasonable and justifiable.

He highlighted his strengths as a buyer—his pre-approved financing and flexibility with the closing date. By presenting himself as a serious and reliable buyer, Jordan made his offer more attractive.

PART III
CLOSING & **MANAGING**

THE DUE DILIGENCE DANCE: AVOIDING COMMON PITFALLS

Alright, let's get into the nitty-gritty of due diligence—the stage where you separate the serious players from the wannabes. Due diligence is like preparing for a high-stakes performance. You've got to nail every step to avoid stepping on any landmines. In real estate, getting this right can make or break your investment. So let's dive in and master this dance.

Preparation: Your Winning Strategy

Before you even think about making an offer, you've got to be prepared. Think of this as your rehearsal. Know your property, your market, and your goals inside out.

- **Market Research:** Start by getting a firm grip on the market. Look at recent sales of similar properties (comps), and understand where the market is heading. This isn't just about numbers; it's about feeling the pulse of the market.

- **Property Analysis:** Dive deep into the property's details. What's its condition? What's it going to cost to bring it up to your standards? Don't just skim the surface—get a professional inspection to uncover those hidden issues that could come back to haunt you.

- **Know Your Goals:** What do you want from this investment? Are you after cash flow, appreciation, or a mix of both? Clarity here is crucial; it'll guide your entire approach.

Physical Inspection: Spotting the Hidden Problems

The physical inspection is your chance to find out if the property is a gem or a money pit.

- **Hire a Pro:** Get a certified home inspector or building engineer who knows their stuff. They'll look at the property from top to bottom and find issues you might miss.

- **Review the Report:** Don't just glance at the inspection report—absorb it. If there are major red flags like structural issues or outdated systems, take note. These will impact your bottom line.

- **Budget for Repairs:** Use the inspection report to estimate repair costs. These aren't just numbers; they're your potential deal-breakers. Make sure they fit into your investment strategy.

Financial Performance: Crunching the Numbers

Let's talk about the numbers—the stuff that either makes or breaks your deal.

- **Historical Financials:** Dig into the property's financial history. Look at past rent rolls, operating expenses, and income statements. This is where you'll find out if the property has been performing like a superstar or just limping along.

- **Project Future Income:** What can you expect to earn from this property? Project future rents based on current market rates and the property's rental history. Factor in potential vacancies and rent increases.

- **Assess Expenses:** Don't overlook the expenses. Review all operating costs and make sure they align with your financial projections. Unexpected expenses can turn a lucrative investment into a financial drain.

Legal Due Diligence: Navigating the Legal Maze

Legal due diligence is your chance to ensure there are no surprises lurking in the fine print.

- **Title Search:** Conduct a thorough title search to make sure the property's title is clean. Look out for liens, encumbrances, or claims that could complicate your ownership.
- **Zoning and Land Use:** Check the zoning regulations and land use policies. Make sure they're in line with your investment plans. You don't want to buy a property only to find out you can't use it as you intended.
- **Review Legal Documents:** Examine all legal documents related to the property, including leases and rental agreements. Ensure there are no ongoing disputes or legal issues that could affect your investment.

Common Pitfalls: What to Watch Out For

Even the best can trip up if they're not careful. Here's what to avoid:

- **Ignoring Inspection Findings:** Don't brush off issues found during the inspection. Major repairs can be costly and affect your investment's profitability. Address these issues head-on.
- **Overlooking Financial Analysis:** Incomplete or inaccurate financial data can lead to poor investment decisions. Ensure you have a clear, accurate understanding of the property's financial performance.

- **Neglecting Legal Matters:** Don't overlook potential legal problems. Unresolved liens or zoning violations can create serious headaches. Thorough legal due diligence is essential.

- **Underestimating Renovation Costs:** Be realistic about renovation costs. Underestimating these can turn a profitable investment into a money pit. Get accurate estimates and factor these into your projections.

Finalizing Your Due Diligence: Making the Call

Once you've gathered all the information, it's time to make your move.

- **Review Findings:** Look at the complete picture from the inspection, financial analysis, and legal review. Ensure the property aligns with your goals and investment criteria.

- **Make an Informed Decision:** Decide whether to proceed, renegotiate, or walk away. Your decision should be based on a thorough understanding of the property and its potential risks and rewards.

Dancing Your Way to Success

Mastering the due diligence dance is about preparation, precision, and avoiding pitfalls. With thorough research, detailed inspections, and careful legal and financial review, you can navigate this complex process and make informed decisions. Remember, due diligence isn't just a checklist—it's your pathway to making smart, successful investments. So get out there, perform the due diligence dance, and secure the deals that set you up for long-term success.

Behind the Price Tag: Stephen's Costly Lesson in Due Diligence

Let me tell you about a client named Stephen, who learned the hard way that due diligence isn't just a formality—it's a necessity.

When Stephen first came to me, he was frustrated, defeated, and looking for a way to recover from what he called "the worst investment of his life." He had recently bought a four-unit multifamily property in Virginia Beach, thinking he'd scored a fantastic deal. The property was in a rapidly developing area, and the price seemed too good to pass up. But as the saying goes, if it seems too good to be true, it probably is.

Stephen had jumped into the purchase without fully understanding what due diligence really meant. He'd relied heavily on the seller's word and a quick once-over from a general home inspector. On the surface, everything seemed fine: the property was in a desirable location, the units were occupied, and the rent roll looked solid. Stephen was eager to start collecting rent checks, so he rushed through the process and closed the deal quickly.

It didn't take long for the problems to start piling up.

The Discovery: Issues Below the Surface

Within a few months, Stephen began receiving complaints from tenants about persistent plumbing issues—leaks that led to water damage and mold. When he finally brought in a specialized contractor to assess the situation, he learned that the plumbing system was outdated and needed a complete overhaul. The cost? Tens of thousands of dollars—money Stephen hadn't budgeted for.

But the plumbing was just the beginning. A deeper inspection revealed that the property's electrical system was also outdated, posing a fire hazard. The roof, which Stephen had assumed was in good condition based on the seller's claims, turned out to be nearing the end of its lifespan. Again, Stephen faced unexpected costs that were rapidly eroding his anticipated profits.

The Financial Fallout: Crunching Unpleasant Numbers

As if the physical problems weren't enough, Stephen discovered financial discrepancies that he had overlooked during the buying process. The rent roll he'd relied on wasn't as solid as it seemed. Two of the four units were rented to tenants who were months behind on payments. The seller had conveniently neglected to mention that these tenants had a history of late payments and evictions.

Stephen also realized that he hadn't accounted for higher-than-expected operating expenses, including utility costs that were much higher than the seller had indicated. The cash flow he'd anticipated quickly turned negative as he scrambled to cover repairs, unpaid rent, and inflated expenses.

The Legal Nightmare: A Costly Oversight

The final blow came when Stephen received a letter from the city about zoning violations. The property, it turned out, wasn't fully compliant with local zoning laws. The previous owner had made unpermitted alterations to the building, which now required costly corrections to bring the property up to code. This legal issue had been sitting there, hidden in plain sight, waiting for someone to find it during the due diligence phase. But Stephen had never looked deeply enough.

The Turnaround: Learning from the Mistakes

When Stephen walked into my office, he was desperate for a solution. He needed help navigating the mess he found himself in. The first thing we did was a thorough analysis of what had gone wrong, starting with the due diligence he had skipped.

We brought in professionals to assess the property properly this time: a licensed home inspector, a structural engineer, a zoning attorney, and an accountant. I walked Stephen through the process, showing him how each of these steps could have saved him from the situation he was in. We worked out a plan to stabilize the property, address the immediate issues, and renegotiate with the tenants. It wasn't easy, and it wasn't cheap, but it was the only way to stop the bleeding.

The Lesson: Due Diligence is Non-Negotiable

Stephen's story is a cautionary tale about the dangers of skipping due diligence. He learned that a good deal isn't just about the price tag—it's about what lies beneath the surface. If you don't take the time to dig deep, to understand exactly what you're buying, you're setting yourself up for potential disaster.

Since then, Stephen has become a diligent investor, never skipping a single step in the due diligence process. He's gone on to make successful investments, but only because he now knows that taking the time upfront can save you from massive headaches and financial loss down the road.

This experience was a tough lesson for Stephen, but it's one he'll never forget—and neither will I. It's why I tell every client: due diligence isn't just about protecting your investment; it's about securing your future.

CLOSING THE DEAL: NAVIGATING THE FINAL STEPS

So, you've found the perfect property, done your due diligence, and negotiated a deal that makes you feel like a rockstar. Now, it's time to close. This is the final stretch, the grand finale where all your hard work comes together. But don't get too comfortable just yet—this stage is packed with crucial steps that need your full attention. Closing a deal isn't just about signing on the dotted line; it's about ensuring everything is in place for a smooth and successful transition. Let's walk through the process so you can close with confidence.

The Closing Checklist: Staying on Top of the Details

The first thing you need is a detailed closing checklist. Think of this as your roadmap to the finish line. It should include every task that needs to be completed before the deal is officially yours. This list will keep you organized and ensure nothing slips through the cracks.

- **Final Walkthrough:** A day or two before closing, schedule a final walkthrough of the property. This isn't just a formality—this is your last chance to ensure the property is in the condition agreed upon in the contract. Check that any repairs have been completed and that nothing has changed since your initial inspection.

- **Review the Closing Disclosure:** The Closing Disclosure is a critical document that outlines all the financial details of your transaction. It will include the loan terms, monthly payments, fees, and closing costs. Review it carefully, compare it to the Loan Estimate you received earlier, and make sure everything matches up. Any discrepancies should be addressed immediately.

- **Secure Homeowners Insurance:** Before closing, you'll need to secure homeowners insurance. This is a requirement for most lenders, and they'll need proof of insurance before they'll release the funds. Shop around for the best rates and coverage to protect your new investment.

Title and Escrow: Ensuring a Smooth Transfer

Title and escrow services play a crucial role in the closing process. They ensure that the property's title is clear and that the funds are properly handled.

- **Title Search:** The title company will perform a title search to confirm that the property's title is clear of any liens, encumbrances, or legal disputes. This is essential because you don't want to inherit any unresolved issues from the previous owner. If any problems arise, they'll need to be resolved before you can close.

- **Title Insurance:** Even with a thorough title search, there's always a small risk that something could be missed. That's where title insurance comes in. This protects you (and your lender) from any potential legal claims against your ownership. It's a one-time fee that provides peace of mind for as long as you own the property.

- **Escrow Account:** The escrow company acts as a neutral third party, holding onto the funds and documents until all conditions of the sale are met. They'll disburse the funds to the seller, pay off any existing liens, and handle other financial aspects of the closing. It's their job to ensure that everything is in order before the property officially changes hands.

Closing Costs: Understanding the Final Expenses

Closing costs can sometimes catch buyers off guard, so it's important to understand what they are and budget for them accordingly. These costs typically range from 2% to 5% of the purchase price and include various fees and expenses.

- **Loan Origination Fee:** This is the fee your lender charges for processing your loan. It's usually a percentage of the loan amount, and it's typically one of the largest closing costs.

- **Appraisal Fee:** If you haven't already paid for the appraisal, this fee will be included in your closing costs. The appraisal ensures the property is worth the amount you're borrowing.

- **Inspection Fees:** If you had any additional inspections (like a termite or radon inspection), these fees will also be included.

- **Attorney Fees:** If you used a real estate attorney to review your documents, their fees will be part of your closing costs.

- **Title Insurance:** The cost of your title insurance policy will be included in your closing costs.

- **Escrow Fees:** The escrow company will charge a fee for handling the closing process, which will be part of your closing costs.

The Closing Meeting: Sealing the Deal

The closing meeting is where all the final paperwork is signed, and the property officially becomes yours. It's usually held at the office of the title company, escrow agent, or your real estate attorney.

- **Bring Necessary Documents:** You'll need to bring a government-issued ID, proof of homeowners insurance, and a cashier's check or wire transfer for the closing costs and down payment. Your lender will provide instructions on how to make the payment.

- **Review and Sign Documents:** During the closing meeting, you'll review and sign a stack of documents, including the deed, mortgage agreement, and various disclosures. Take your time and read each document carefully. If you have any questions, don't hesitate to ask—this is a significant financial transaction, and you want to be sure you understand everything.

- **Receive the Keys:** Once all the paperwork is signed and the funds are transferred, you'll receive the keys to your new property. Congratulations—you're now a property owner!

Post-Closing: What Happens Next?

After the closing meeting, there are still a few important steps to complete.

- **Record the Deed:** The title company will record the deed with the local county recorder's office. This officially transfers ownership of the property to you.

- **Move In:** Now that the property is officially yours, it's time to move in or start any planned renovations. If you're renting out the property, begin the process of finding tenants or introducing yourself to the existing ones.

- **Set Up Utilities and Services:** Don't forget to set up utilities, internet, and any other services you'll need at the property. It's a good idea to handle this before you move in to ensure everything is ready when you arrive.

Closing with Confidence

Closing a real estate deal is a complex process, but with the right preparation and guidance, you can navigate it successfully. Remember, every step is crucial—from the final walkthrough to the closing meeting. By staying organized, asking questions, and double-checking everything, you'll ensure a smooth transition from buyer to owner. This is the moment where all your hard work pays off, and you can finally take a deep breath and celebrate your new investment.

Rushed to Ruin: David's Costly Oversights in the Final Steps

Let me share a story about a client of mine, who I'll call David. David was a smart guy, sharp as a tack, and had a natural talent for spotting good investment opportunities. He'd found a great property in Norfolk, Virginia—a beautiful, historic single-family home that he planned to renovate and flip. The numbers checked out, the neighborhood was up-and-coming, and everything seemed to be lining up perfectly. But David made one critical mistake: he neglected the final steps in the closing process.

David was excited—maybe too excited. He'd already lined up contractors, started picking out materials for the renovation, and was envisioning the huge profits he'd make from the flip. So when it came time for the closing process, he was eager to get it over with and move on to the next phase. Unfortunately, that eagerness led to some costly oversights.

Skipping the Final Walkthrough

One of the biggest mistakes David made was skipping the final walkthrough. He was in such a rush to close that he didn't take the time to go back to the property and ensure everything was in the condition agreed upon in the contract. He trusted that the seller had completed all the necessary repairs and didn't feel the need to check things out one last time.

Big mistake.

When David finally got the keys and went to the property to start the renovations, he was in for a nasty surprise. The roof, which the seller had agreed to repair, hadn't been touched. Not only that, but the plumbing issues that had been flagged during the inspection were still there, lurking in the walls. What should have been a quick renovation turned into a money pit, with unexpected repair costs eating into David's budget.

Overlooking the Closing Disclosure

David's second mistake was not thoroughly reviewing the Closing Disclosure. This document outlined all the financial details of the transaction, including loan terms, fees, and closing costs. But David was so focused on the big picture that he glossed over the details.

When he finally took a closer look—after the deal had closed—he realized that some of the fees were higher than he had expected. The lender had included additional charges that David hadn't anticipated, and the closing costs ended up being significantly more than he had budgeted for. If he had caught this earlier, he might have been able to negotiate or at least prepare for the extra expenses.

Insurance Oversight

David also neglected to secure the right homeowners insurance before closing. He had assumed that his existing policy on another property would cover the new one, but that wasn't the case. The lender needed proof of insurance specific to the new property, and because David hadn't provided it in time, there was a delay in the closing process.

This delay caused a ripple effect: his contractors, who were ready to start work immediately after closing, had to be rescheduled, pushing the renovation timeline back by several weeks. In the world of real estate, time is money, and this delay cost David more than just a few weeks—it cost him potential profits as market conditions shifted slightly during the delay.

The Title Trouble

Perhaps the most significant oversight was with the title. The title company had flagged a minor lien on the property during their search, something that could have been easily resolved before closing. But David, in his rush to get things done, ignored it, thinking it wouldn't be a big deal.

It was.

That minor lien turned into a major headache when it prevented him from selling the property as quickly as he had planned. Clearing up the issue took months of legal wrangling and additional costs that ate into his profits. What should have been a quick flip turned into a drawn-out process that left David frustrated and financially strained.

The Lesson: Finish Strong

David's story is a prime example of how important it is to finish strong in real estate. The final steps in the closing process aren't just formalities—they're critical to ensuring that your investment is secure and that there are no unpleasant surprises waiting for you after the deal is done.

If David had taken the time to do the final walkthrough, carefully review the Closing Disclosure, secure the right insurance, and resolve the title issue before closing, he could have saved himself a lot of trouble and money. Instead, his rush to the finish line led to costly mistakes that turned what should have been a profitable investment into a cautionary tale.

Now, whenever I'm working with clients on a deal, I always share David's story. It's a reminder that in real estate, it's not over until it's over, and the final steps are just as important as everything that came before.

PROPERTY MANAGEMENT 101: ENSURING A SMOOTH OPERATION

Alright, let's dive into the high-stakes world of property management. Think of it as being the CEO of a small empire—it's not just about collecting rents; it's about steering the ship right to keep everything sleek, efficient, and profitable. Whether you're managing a charming little duplex or a towering high-rise, mastering property management is key to turning those real estate investments into gold mines.

The Role of a Property Manager

As a property manager, you're in the driver's seat. Your job is to keep the property running like a well-oiled machine—happy tenants, pristine maintenance, and the finances tight and right. Here's the breakdown:

- **Tenant Relations:** This is where your charm kicks in. Building great relationships with your tenants isn't just being nice—it's strategic. Happy tenants mean longer stays, fewer vacancies, and less drama.

- **Maintenance and Upkeep:** This is about protecting your investment. Regular check-ups and quick fixes keep a molehill from becoming a mountain—basically, it saves you money in the long run and keeps your property looking top-notch.

- **Financial Management:** You've got to have your numbers dialed in. Efficient rent collection, meticulous bookkeeping, and savvy budgeting are what keep the cash flowing and your investments profitable.

- **Legal Know-how:** Staying on top of landlord-tenant laws and regulations isn't just good practice—it's essential to avoid costly legal battles and fines.

Setting Up for Success

Get the infrastructure right, and you're halfway to success. Here's how you make sure your property management is set to "win":

- **Tech Tools:** Leveraging technology can transform how you manage properties. Think digital—use property management software like AppFolio or Buildium to automate everything from tenant screening to rent collection and maintenance requests.

- **The Tenant Handbook:** Create a go-to guide for your tenants. This isn't just a list of do's and don'ts; it's the blueprint to living in your property. It sets clear expectations and helps avoid misunderstandings.

- **Maintenance Calendar:** Keep a calendar for regular maintenance. It's like a health check-up schedule but for your property. Regular care keeps costly emergencies at bay.

- **Trusted Contractors:** Have a speed dial list of rockstar contractors. Reliable plumbers, electricians, and handymen who deliver quality work on time can save you a ton of hassle.

Tenant Screening & Lease Mastery

Here's where you need to be sharp. Choosing the right tenant is like casting for a blockbuster movie—you need a star who fits the role perfectly.

- **Screening Process:** Implement a bulletproof screening process. Credit checks, background checks, employment verification—you need it all to ensure you're getting someone reliable and responsible.

- **Lease Agreements:** Your lease is your contract—it's got to be ironclad. Make sure it's clear, comprehensive, and legally sound. Cover everything from the length of the tenancy to the specifics of the deposit and maintenance responsibilities.

- **Move-In/Move-Out Protocols:** Have clear protocols for move-ins and move-outs. Detailed inspections and documented conditions of the property ensure that there are no disputes over security deposits when it's time to part ways.

Handling the Unexpected

Even the best-laid plans can hit snags—be ready for anything.

- **Emergency Preparedness:** Have an emergency action plan. Whether it's a natural disaster or a burst pipe at 2 AM, knowing what to do immediately can mitigate damage and costs.

- **Proactive Inspections:** Regularly inspect the property yourself. Don't wait for tenants to tell you something's wrong. Finding and fixing issues early can prevent major headaches down the line.

Financial Wizardry

This is where you make sure the money keeps rolling in.

- **Rent Collection Systems:** Set up a seamless rent collection system. Online payments are the way to go—they're convenient, fast, and you don't have to chase anyone for checks.

- **Budget Like a Pro:** Keep a keen eye on your operating expenses. Know where every dollar is going, and make sure you're always getting the best deals for services and repairs.

- **Regular Reporting:** Keep detailed financial records and regularly review your income and expenses. This not only helps you stay on top of your financial game but also makes tax time a breeze.

Be the Boss of Your Property Empire

Great property management is about attention to detail, being proactive, and always staying a step ahead. It's about turning challenges into opportunities and properties into profitable ventures. With the right approach, tools, and attitude, you can not only manage your properties effectively but also turn them into the stars of your real estate portfolio. So, strap in, get organized, and take charge—it's time to make your mark in the world of property management!

Sophia's Shift from DIY Landlord to Professional Property Management

Let me tell you about a client named Sophia, who thought she could handle the whirlwind world of property management on her own. She had a sharp eye for investment properties and snagged three small apartment buildings in a hot part of town. At first, she was all about cutting costs and boosting her bottom line, so she skipped on professional property management. "How hard can it be?" she thought.

DIY Property Management: Sophia's Early Wins

Initially, Sophia was on a roll. She managed tenant screenings, handled the leases, and even took on the odd repair job herself. She felt invincible, saving money left and right, and truly owning the role of a hands-on property mogul.

The Wake-Up Call: Challenges Pile Up

But soon, the real challenges of property management began to rear their ugly heads. Sophia was bombarded with maintenance calls at all hours, tenant complaints multiplied, and the paperwork started piling up. Rent collection became her monthly nightmare, with late payments and some tenants playing hide and seek come due date.

- **Tenant Troubles:** Not all tenants were the dream renters she had hoped for. One was a constant source of noise complaints, while another turned late payments into an art form. Sophia's initial screenings missed critical red flags that a pro would have caught.

- **Maintenance Mayhem:** With no reliable contractor on speed dial, every leak or electrical issue became an emergency. Costs spiraled, especially after a major plumbing disaster turned one of the buildings into an accidental water park—ouch!

- **Legal Labyrinth:** When Sophia tried to evict a non-paying tenant, she hit a legal wall. Turns out, her DIY lease agreements were about as watertight as a sieve, and her eviction process was off track from the get-go.

Sophia Calls for Backup: Enter the Pros

Realizing her investments were turning into money pits, Sophia came to me, worn out and ready for a change. I steered her towards a top-notch property management company known for turning chaotic rentals into well-oiled machines.

The Transformation: Smooth Sailing with Professional Management

The property management team took the reins and revolutionized Sophia's approach:

- **Top-Tier Tenant Screening:** They implemented a rigorous screening process that filled Sophia's buildings with reliable, rent-paying tenants.
- **Maintenance Network:** They brought in a crew of ace contractors who fixed ongoing issues and set up a regular maintenance schedule—no more emergency calls for Sophia.
- **Legal Tightening:** They overhauled the lease agreements and handled all legal compliance, turning Sophia's legal labyrinth into a walk in the park.

The Payoff: Stability and Growth

With the pros at the helm, Sophia's properties became the investment dream she had envisioned. Tenant turnover dropped, rental income flowed in like clockwork, and her buildings were in the best shape ever. Most importantly, Sophia could finally sleep at night, knowing her properties and her profits were in good hands.

The Big Lesson: Penny Wise, Pound Foolish

Sophia's journey is a masterclass in why cutting corners in property management is a gamble that's not worth the risk. It taught her that investing a little in great property management can save a fortune in the long run and turn potential disasters into booming successes.

Remember, folks, in the high-stakes game of real estate, being savvy doesn't just mean saving pennies—it means investing in peace of mind and profitability. Don't be like early-days Sophia; manage your properties like the prime real estate empire they are meant to be.

MAXIMIZING RETURNS: STRATEGIES FOR PROFIT GROWTH

Welcome to the high-octane world of real estate, where playing it safe doesn't make you the big bucks! If you're ready to turbocharge your investments and see those profits soar, you're in the right place. This chapter isn't about coasting along; it's about pushing the pedal to the metal and maximizing every single asset in your portfolio. Let's dive into the strategies that will not only boost your income but also transform you into a real estate mogul.

Squeeze Every Dollar from Your Rentals

First things first, let's pump up that rental income. It's not just about collecting checks; it's about maximizing every unit to its full potential:

- **Market-Smart Pricing:** Are you leaving money on the table? Regularly check the pulse of your local rental market to ensure your rates are on point. If you're not riding the wave of market rates, you're not maximizing your income.
- **Vacancy is the Enemy:** Every empty apartment is a missed opportunity. Amp up your marketing game to keep

those units filled. Use dazzling photos, virtual tours, and irresistible property descriptions to hook prospective tenants.

- **Luxury Upgrades:** Small luxuries make a big difference. Think stainless steel appliances, granite countertops, or even smart home features. These can justify higher rent and attract tenants who are willing to pay top dollar for top-tier amenities.

Trim the Fat on Expenses

Boosting profits isn't just about increasing income; it's also about slashing unnecessary expenses. Get lean and mean with operational costs:

- **Preventative Maintenance:** Stay ahead of the curve with regular maintenance checks. It's like a fitness routine for your property—keeping it in peak condition reduces costly breakdowns.

- **Go Green to Save Green:** Invest in energy-efficient upgrades. LED lighting, eco-friendly appliances, and solar panels can cut down utility costs and appeal to environmentally conscious tenants.

- **Automate Everything Possible:** Time is money, and modern property management software can save loads of both. Automate tasks like rent collection, tenant screening, and maintenance requests to streamline operations and cut down on administrative costs.

Capitalize on Tax Benefits

Don't let the tax man scare you. Real estate is loaded with tax advantages that can significantly enhance your cash flow:

- **Depreciation is Your Friend:** Accelerate depreciation expenses to shield income from taxes, putting more money back in your pocket each year.

- **Cost Segregation Studies:** Get granular with your depreciation. A cost segregation study can speed up depreciation deductions, improving cash flow and reducing taxable income early in the property's life.

- **Stay Informed on Tax Credits:** Keep your ear to the ground for any local or federal tax incentives for property improvements or energy efficiency upgrades.

Smart Refinancing

Interest rates are like the weather; they change. When they drop, it's time to refinance:

- **Better Mortgage Rates:** Locking in a lower interest rate through refinancing can reduce your monthly payments and boost your bottom line.

- **Leverage Equity:** Consider a cash-out refinance to pull cash from your property's equity. Use that capital to invest in more properties, renovations, or to diversify your investment portfolio.

Upgrade and Enhance

Investing back into your properties can significantly increase their value and your rental income:

- **Curb Appeal Matters:** First impressions are everything. A fresh coat of paint, landscaped gardens, and modern signage can make your property stand out from the crowd.

- **Functional Overhauls:** Modernize outdated kitchens and bathrooms. These renovations not only increase property value but also make your listings irresistible.

- **Adding Units or Expanding:** If zoning laws permit, consider adding additional units or expanding existing ones to increase your rental income exponentially.

Cutting-Edge Tech for Market Analysis

Stay ahead of the game with technology that offers real-time insights and forecasts:

- **Real Estate Analytics Platforms:** Use advanced platforms to get actionable insights on property valuations, rent trends, and market dynamics.

- **Predictive Analytics:** Implement tools that use AI to predict market trends, helping you buy or sell at the perfect time.

Become a Real Estate Tycoon

Maximizing returns in real estate is about being bold, innovative, and strategic. By optimizing rental income, cutting costs, leveraging tax breaks, refinancing at opportune moments, and continuously upgrading your properties, you set the stage for unmatched profitability. Remember, in the world of real estate, the bold take the prizes. So step up, make smart choices, and watch your profits soar to new heights!

Fast Track to Fallout: Marcus's Lessons in Strategic Real Estate Investment

I'll share a story about a client of Marcus, the overeager real estate enthusiast who thought he could outsmart the market—spoiler alert: the market wasn't amused. Marcus, armed with more enthusiasm than experience, decided that he was going to be a real estate mogul overnight. His plan? Buy as much as he could, as fast as he could, with as much borrowed money as his credit could handle. What could possibly go wrong, right?

The Race to Buy Everything

Marcus kicked off his empire-building by scooping up a duplex, flipping it, and making a tidy profit. Feeling invincible, he then grabbed three more properties in record time. His strategy was like trying to play Monopoly on a rocket ship—fast, furious, and a bit reckless.

Due Diligence? I Don't Know Her

In his rush, Marcus treated due diligence like it was a suggestion rather than a requirement. One property was so cheap it made dollar store deals look expensive. He missed that it was smack dab in the middle of the neighborhood's "tour de crime" and declining faster than my patience in a traffic jam.

The Great Rent Illusion

For another gem in his collection, Marcus decided to slap some paint on, throw in a few IKEA fixtures, and charge rents that would make a Manhattan landlord blush. The problem? He was in an area where residents thought wine pairings were choosing which soda goes with pizza. Needless to say, the apartments stayed emptier than a politician's promises.

Operating Costs? What's That?

Marcus, in his infinite optimism, figured he could run his properties on a budget tighter than skinny jeans after Thanksgiving dinner. Turns out, old buildings eat cash faster than kids eat candy. The repair bills piled up like my fan mail.

Zoning Laws Enter the Chat

And oh, the zoning debacle—Marcus bought a property dreaming of converting it into a bustling multi-family complex. Too bad the local zoning laws were more restrictive than my high school dress code. His dreams hit a legal wall, and the property had to be offloaded like last season's fashion.

The Financial Cliff

When the market dipped, Marcus found himself over-leveraged and under-prepared. Properties underwater, he was bleeding cash like a sieve. In a desperate move, he had to fire-sale two properties, which felt about as good as stepping on a Lego barefoot.

The Comeback Kid

That's when Marcus came to me, tail between his legs, looking for a lifeline. We strapped on our helmets and got to work. We trimmed the fat, tightened up operations, and got real about pricing. I taught him that real estate isn't a sprint; it's more like a marathon—sometimes through a mud pit, but a marathon nonetheless.

Lessons from the School of Hard Knocks

Marcus's comedic misadventures in real estate taught him some hard-knock lessons: due diligence is non-negotiable, understanding your market is crucial, and realistic pricing is key. Oh, and maybe, just maybe, trying to become a real estate titan overnight is about as smart as eating soup with a fork.

From then on, Marcus approached his investments with a mix of cautious strategy and informed optimism, turning his once chaotic portfolio into a well-oiled profit machine. He learned that in real estate, the tortoise often beats the hare, and slow and steady wins the race (especially when the race is uphill, in the snow, both ways).

Marcus's story is a reminder that while real estate can turn dreams into reality, it can just as quickly turn a comedy of errors into a tragedy if you're not careful. So take it from Marcus: measure twice, cut once, and maybe slow down on the empire-building until you've got your real estate legs under you.

PART IV
EXPANDING & **REFLECTING**

OVERCOMING CHALLENGES: WHAT TO DO WHEN THINGS **GO WRONG**

Challenges are inevitable. Even the most experienced investors and agents encounter bumps along the road. It's not about avoiding these obstacles—because, let's be real, they're going to happen—it's about how you respond to them that defines your success. This chapter is your roadmap for navigating the inevitable storms, so when things go wrong, you're not just surviving—you're thriving.

The Reality of Real Estate: Embracing the Unexpected

First, let's get something straight: in real estate, Murphy's Law is always in play. If something can go wrong, it eventually will. Whether it's a deal falling through, unexpected repairs, tenant issues, or market downturns, these challenges are part of the game. The key is to expect the unexpected and develop the resilience and tools needed to handle whatever comes your way.

Dealing with Financial Hiccups

Financial challenges can range from unexpected expenses to

cash flow problems, and they can derail even the best-laid plans if not managed correctly. Here's how to navigate these financial minefields:

- **Create a Cash Reserve:** The first rule of thumb is to always have a cash reserve. This safety net allows you to cover unexpected expenses like major repairs, vacancies, or sudden market downturns. Aim for at least three to six months' worth of operating expenses.

- **Reevaluate Your Budget:** If you're facing financial strain, take a hard look at your budget. Cut non-essential expenses and look for areas where you can tighten your belt. This might include renegotiating contracts with vendors, delaying non-critical upgrades, or adjusting your marketing spend.

- **Refinance or Refinance Again:** If mortgage payments are becoming a burden, consider refinancing to lower your interest rate or extend your loan term. Just make sure the benefits outweigh the costs.

- **Emergency Financing:** Explore options for emergency financing, like lines of credit or hard money loans. While these shouldn't be your first choice due to higher interest rates, they can provide quick cash when you're in a bind.

Handling Property Damage and Maintenance Nightmares

Property damage can range from minor issues like leaky faucets to catastrophic events like fires or floods. Knowing how to respond swiftly and effectively can save you time, money, and stress.

- **Routine Inspections:** Preventative maintenance is your best defense against unexpected repairs. Regularly inspect your properties to catch small issues before they turn into big problems. Seasonal inspections are especially important to prepare for weather-related challenges.

- **Develop a Reliable Network:** Build a network of trusted contractors and maintenance professionals who can respond quickly when issues arise. Having a go-to team means you won't be scrambling to find help in an emergency.

- **Insurance Savvy:** Ensure your properties are adequately insured for a variety of potential risks. Understand the specifics of your policies, including what's covered and what's not, and consider additional coverage for things like floods, earthquakes, or other region-specific risks.

- **Document Everything:** Keep detailed records of all maintenance and repairs. Not only does this help with accountability and budgeting, but it also protects you in case of disputes with tenants or contractors.

Tenant Troubles: Managing the People Side of Real Estate

Tenants can be both your greatest asset and your biggest headache. From late payments to lease violations, managing tenants effectively is crucial to maintaining a smooth operation.

- **Clear Communication:** Establish clear, consistent communication from the start. Make sure tenants understand the terms of their lease, the rules of the property, and the procedures for reporting issues.

- **Strict Screening Process:** To minimize tenant-related challenges, implement a thorough screening process. This should include credit checks, background checks, employment verification, and references. A little extra time upfront can save you a lot of trouble later.

- **Prompt Conflict Resolution:** When tenant issues arise, address them immediately. Whether it's a noise complaint, a maintenance request, or a lease violation, quick action shows tenants that you take their concerns seriously and helps prevent small issues from escalating.

- **Know When to Evict:** If a tenant consistently violates their lease or fails to pay rent, don't hesitate to start the eviction process. It's not a pleasant task, but sometimes it's necessary to protect your investment. Just be sure to follow all legal procedures to avoid complications.

Navigating Market Downturns

Market downturns can be one of the most challenging aspects of real estate. Whether it's a local economic slump or a broader recession, knowing how to navigate tough times is essential.

- **Diversify Your Portfolio:** One of the best ways to protect yourself against market downturns is to diversify your real estate portfolio. Invest in different types of properties (residential, commercial, multifamily) and in various locations to spread your risk.

- **Focus on Cash Flow:** During a downturn, cash flow is king. Focus on properties that generate reliable rental income rather than those that rely on appreciation. This steady income can help you weather the storm.

- **Adjust Rent Strategically:** If vacancies increase, consider adjusting your rent slightly to attract tenants. While you don't want to undercut your profits, a small reduction in rent is better than having a property sit vacant for months.

- **Stay Informed:** Keep an eye on economic indicators and market trends. Understanding what's happening in the broader economy can help you anticipate changes and adjust your strategy accordingly.

Legal and Regulatory Challenges

Legal issues can arise from a variety of sources—tenant disputes, zoning changes, or regulatory compliance. Being proactive and informed is key to avoiding costly legal battles.

- **Stay Up-to-Date on Laws:** Real estate laws and regulations are constantly evolving. Make it a habit to stay informed about changes in landlord-tenant laws, zoning ordinances, and building codes that could affect your properties.

- **Consult with Legal Professionals:** When in doubt, consult with a real estate attorney. Whether it's reviewing contracts, handling disputes, or navigating complex legal issues, having a professional on your side can save you from costly mistakes.

- **Document Everything:** Good record-keeping is your best defense in legal disputes. Document all interactions with tenants, contractors, and regulatory agencies. Keep copies of leases, contracts, and correspondence in case you need them for legal proceedings.

Emotional Resilience: Keeping Your Cool Under Pressure

Real estate can be a rollercoaster, and it's easy to get overwhelmed when things go wrong. Maintaining your emotional resilience is crucial to navigating challenges effectively.

- **Stay Calm and Objective:** When faced with a problem, take a step back and assess the situation objectively. Panicking or making decisions out of frustration can lead to mistakes. Take a deep breath, analyze the facts, and develop a plan of action.

- **Build a Support System:** Whether it's a mentor, a fellow investor, or a real estate group, having a support system can provide valuable advice and perspective. Sometimes just talking through a problem with someone else can help you find a solution.

- **Learn from Mistakes:** Every challenge is an opportunity to learn. When things go wrong, reflect on what happened and how you can prevent it in the future. This mindset not only helps you grow as an investor but also makes you more resilient.

The Power of Adaptability

The ability to adapt is one of the most valuable skills in real estate. Markets change, tenants come and go, and unexpected challenges will always arise. The investors who thrive are the ones who can pivot quickly and adjust their strategies to fit new circumstances.

- **Be Open to Change:** Don't get stuck in your ways. If a strategy isn't working, be willing to try something new. Whether it's adjusting your investment focus, exploring new markets, or adopting new technologies, staying flexible is key to long-term success.

- **Continuously Educate Yourself:** Real estate is a constantly evolving field, and the most successful investors are lifelong learners. Attend seminars, read industry publications, and stay curious about new trends and opportunities.

Thriving Through Challenges

In real estate, challenges are not just inevitable—they're essential. They push you to think creatively, adapt to new circumstances, and become a better investor. The key is to approach these challenges not with dread but with determination. By building a strong foundation, staying informed, and maintaining emotional resilience, you can turn obstacles into opportunities and ensure that when things go wrong, you're ready to make them right.

So, the next time you hit a bump in the road, remember: every challenge is a chance to grow. Embrace it, tackle it head-on, and use it as a stepping stone to even greater success. In the world of real estate, it's not the challenges you face that define you—it's how you overcome them.

Turning Turbulence into Triumph: Taylor's Guide to Conquering Real Estate Challenges

Let me tell you about Taylor, a real estate investor who faced a series of challenges that could have derailed even the most seasoned professionals. Taylor's journey is a prime example of turning adversity into opportunity, and it's a testament to resilience and strategic thinking in the world of real estate.

The Bold Beginning

Taylor began investing in real estate with a single property—a modest duplex in a burgeoning neighborhood. The initial months were promising, with stable rental income and a growing property value. Energized by this success, Taylor decided to scale up, acquiring several more properties in quick succession. Everything was on the up and up until, well, it wasn't.

Challenge #1: The Market Shift

Just as Taylor was gearing up for expansion, the local real estate market took an unexpected downturn. Property values dropped, and rental demand fell. Taylor's newly acquired properties, once seen as golden opportunities, were now struggling with high vacancies and dwindling rental income.

The Strategy: Taylor didn't panic. Instead, they took a step back and conducted a thorough market analysis. Taylor discovered that while the market was down, there were emerging opportunities in different neighborhoods. By diversifying into more stable areas with lower vacancy rates, Taylor managed to stabilize the portfolio. They adjusted rental prices to be competitive but still sustainable and focused on properties with consistent demand.

Challenge #2: The Renovation Nightmare

One of Taylor's properties, an old multifamily building, required extensive renovations. Taylor had budgeted carefully, but unforeseen issues emerged: structural problems, outdated plumbing, and electrical code violations. The renovation costs skyrocketed, and what was supposed to be a straightforward project turned into a financial quagmire. The Strategy: Taylor approached this challenge with a problem-solving mindset. They immediately sought advice from a trusted contractor and a financial advisor. Together, they re-evaluated the renovation plan and prioritized essential repairs. By breaking the project into phases and managing cash flow carefully, Taylor mitigated the impact of the cost overruns. They also found cost-effective solutions for some of the issues and negotiated with vendors for better rates.

Challenge #3: Tenant Turmoil

Taylor's properties, particularly those in less stable neighborhoods, began to experience issues with tenants—late payments, lease violations, and even property damage. It was clear that tenant management was becoming a significant challenge.

The Strategy: Taylor took a proactive approach by improving tenant screening processes and implementing a more stringent application review. They also invested in tenant relations, offering incentives for on-time payments and addressing tenant concerns promptly. Taylor set up a comprehensive property management system that automated rent collection, maintenance requests, and communication, significantly reducing tenant-related issues and improving overall property management efficiency.

Challenge #4: Legal Hurdles

A major legal issue emerged when Taylor faced a zoning dispute with one of their properties, which had been intended for a use that was later deemed non-compliant with updated local zoning laws. The legal battle was time-consuming and costly.

The Strategy: Taylor immediately sought legal counsel and worked closely with the attorney to navigate the zoning regulations. They participated in community meetings to understand the local concerns and negotiated a compromise that involved making minor adjustments to the property use. By staying informed and engaged, Taylor not only resolved the zoning issue but also built a positive relationship with the local community, which proved beneficial in the long run.

The Comeback

Through these challenges, Taylor's resilience and strategic approach paid off. The diversified portfolio started to show stability, the renovated property eventually became a high-performing asset, and tenant management improved significantly. Taylor's ability to adapt, manage resources effectively, and make informed decisions turned a series of potential setbacks into a successful comeback.

Lessons Learned

Taylor's journey highlights several key lessons:

- **Market Research is Crucial:** Understanding market trends and being prepared to pivot is essential for long-term success.
- **Budget for the Unexpected:** Always have a buffer for unforeseen costs and be ready to reallocate resources as needed.
- **Effective Property Management:** Implementing strong tenant screening and management practices can save time and money.
- **Seek Professional Help:** Consulting with experts, whether in construction, legal matters, or financial planning, can provide valuable insights and solutions.

Taylor's story is a powerful example of how challenges, while daunting, can lead to growth and success when approached with the right mindset and strategies. It's a reminder that in real estate, resilience and adaptability are key components of long-term achievement.

BUILDING A PORTFOLIO: EXPANDING YOUR INVESTMENT HORIZONS

Alright, so you've got your first property under your belt, and you're feeling pretty good about yourself. You're collecting rent checks, maybe dealing with the occasional tenant issue, but overall, life's good. But here's the thing: one property isn't going to get you that private jet, the beach house, or the freedom to say, "I'm done working for the rest of my life." Nope. To get there, you need to build a portfolio —a glorious, diversified empire of real estate assets that scream, "I'm a serious player in this game."

So, let's talk about expanding your investment horizons. Buckle up, because this ride is about to get interesting.

The One is Not Enough: Why You Need More Properties

Let's get something straight: owning one property is like dipping your toes in the water. It's cute, but we're here to cannonball into the deep end. You need more properties, and not just because it's fun to tell people, "Oh, I own a few places." (Okay, maybe a little bit for that reason.) But seriously, a portfolio gives you:

- **Diversification:** If one property tanks because the tenants decided to start an underground fight club in the basement, you're not sunk. Your other properties keep the cash flowing.

- **Scalability:** More properties mean more income, more appreciation, and yes, more leverage to buy even more properties. It's like Monopoly, but with actual money.

- **Security:** A diversified portfolio is your safety net. If the market shifts or one area takes a hit, your overall risk is spread out.

Know Your Style: What Kind of Investor Are You?

Before you start snapping up properties like they're going out of style, you need to know what kind of investor you are. Are you a flipper, a holder, a developer? It's important to get this right because buying a high-maintenance Victorian in the suburbs when you're more of a sleek condo-in-the-city kind of person is a recipe for stress (and potentially, a mental breakdown).

- **The Buy-and-Hold Pro:** You're in it for the long haul. You love the idea of monthly cash flow, property appreciation, and slow, steady growth. You're the tortoise in the real estate race, and let me tell you, tortoises do pretty well.

- **The Flipper Extraordinaire:** You live for the thrill of the hunt and the makeover montage. You buy properties that need some TLC, fix them up, and flip them faster than you can say "open house." It's high risk, high reward, and you're here for the adrenaline.

- **The Developer Visionary:** You're not afraid of getting your hands dirty—figuratively, of course. You buy land, build something spectacular, and sell it for a premium. You're creating the future, one blueprint at a time.

Location, Location, Location: The Golden Rule of Real Estate

You've heard it a million times (preferably in Part II of this book) because it's true. Location is everything. But here's the kicker: you don't need to buy properties in your backyard. In fact, expanding your portfolio might mean looking outside your comfort zone. Think different cities, states, or even countries.

- **The Local Legend:** You know your city like the back of your hand, and you've got connections that make property deals smoother than a luxury leather couch. Sticking local can be great, especially if you're hands-on.

- **The National Nomad:** You're not afraid to hop on a plane to check out a hot market across the country. Whether it's a booming tech hub or a hidden gem in the Midwest, you're there before everyone else realizes it's the next big thing.

- **The Global Guru:** You think big—really big. International properties, anyone? Sure, there's more paperwork, more laws to navigate, but the potential payoff? Massive. Plus, it gives you an excuse to "work" from a beachfront villa in Bali.

Financing Your Empire: Playing the Leverage Game

Here's a secret: most successful real estate investors don't pay for properties outright. They use other people's money—namely, the bank's. Leveraging your investments means you can buy more properties with less cash upfront. It's like a cheat code for real estate success.

- **Conventional Loans:** The bread and butter of real estate financing. Good credit, a solid down payment, and you're in business.

- **Private Money:** Got a rich uncle? Or maybe you know some investors looking for a good return? Private money is all about networking and convincing people you're worth betting on.

- **Hard Money Loans:** High interest, short terms, but quick cash. Perfect for flips, but not for the faint of heart. These loans are the Red Bull of real estate financing—fast, effective, but don't make it a habit.

- **Portfolio Loans:** Once you've got a few properties, portfolio loans bundle them together. It's like getting a wholesale deal on real estate financing.

Managing the Madness: Keeping Your Portfolio in Check

As you add properties to your empire, things can get chaotic—fast. Tenants, maintenance, taxes, financing, you name it. If you're not careful, your portfolio can go from a gold mine to a minefield.

- **Property Management:** Unless you enjoy 3 AM calls about leaky faucets, hire a property manager. They handle the day-to-day, so you can focus on expanding your empire, not fixing toilets.

- **Automate Everything:** Use property management software to keep track of rents, repairs, leases, and everything in between. Automation is your best friend—embrace it.

- **Regular Reviews:** Don't set it and forget it. Regularly review your portfolio's performance. What's making money? What's not? Be ready to sell off underperforming properties and reinvest in new opportunities.

The Long Game: Planning for the Future

Building a portfolio isn't about getting rich quick—it's about building wealth over time. Real estate is a long game, and patience is key. But with the right strategy, the rewards are massive.

- **Reinvest Profits:** Don't take your profits and buy a sports car (well, not all of it). Reinvest into new properties or upgrades to existing ones. This is how you grow exponentially.
- **Think Legacy:** What's your end game? Whether it's leaving a legacy for your kids, funding a foundation, or just living the high life, keep your ultimate goals in mind. It helps guide your decisions today.
- **Stay Educated:** Real estate is always changing. Markets shift, new laws come into play, technology advances. Stay ahead by continuously educating yourself—seminars, books, podcasts, you name it. The more you know, the better you'll play the game.

Building Your Real Estate Empire

Expanding your real estate portfolio is the key to true wealth in this game. It's not just about collecting properties; it's about strategic growth, smart management, and playing the long game. Remember, building an empire doesn't happen overnight. It takes time, patience, and a whole lot of hustle. But if you're in it for the long haul, the sky's the limit.

So, get out there, think big, and start building that portfolio like the real estate mogul you're destined to be. Because in this business, the more you own, the more you earn—and there's no better feeling than knowing you're not just in the game, you're dominating it.

From Fixer-Uppers to Fortune: Emily's Hilarious Journey to Real Estate Success

Let me tell you about my client, Emily, who went from owning a single, slightly shabby rental property to building a real estate portfolio that would make even the Monopoly guy jealous. Emily started off like so many first-time investors—full of ambition, armed with Google search results, and a dream of making it big in real estate. But unlike most, Emily wasn't content with just one property. Oh no, she had her eyes set on building an empire, one slightly questionable fixer-upper at a time.

The Humble Beginnings: A Rough Diamond in the Rough

Emily's first purchase was a classic—an old duplex in a neighborhood that was "up-and-coming" (translation: it might come up in a decade or so). The place had charm—if by charm you mean creaky floors, wallpaper from the '70s, and a smell that could only be described as "vintage." But Emily saw potential. She rolled up her sleeves, learned how to swing a hammer (and not her thumb), and got to work.

After a lot of DIY YouTube videos and a few too many late-night trips to Home Depot, Emily turned that duplex into a rentable space that tenants actually wanted to live in. It wasn't the Ritz, but it was cozy. And most importantly, it was cash flow positive.

The Expansion Plan: Go Big or Go Home (With More Properties)

With her first successful rental under her belt, Emily got the bug—the real estate bug. It's like regular enthusiasm but with more spreadsheets and fewer weekends. She realized that one property wasn't going to get her to that beach house in the Bahamas, so she started looking for her next investment.

Emily was smart. She didn't just jump at the first listing that popped up. She dug deep into the local market, ran the numbers, and, most importantly, asked herself the critical question: "Would I want to live here?" (The answer was often a resounding no, which meant it was perfect for renting out.)

Emily's next purchase was a triplex in a neighborhood that had just enough gentrification to attract young professionals but still enough grit to keep the purchase price reasonable. She negotiated like a pro, securing a deal that left even the seller wondering if they'd somehow missed a zero on the price.

The Challenges: Of Course, It Wasn't All Sunshine and Rent Checks

But let's not pretend it was all smooth sailing. Building a portfolio isn't just about collecting properties like they're Pokémon cards. Emily faced her fair share of challenges. There was the time a pipe burst in the middle of the night, turning one of her units into an impromptu indoor pool. Or the tenant who decided that "no pets" actually meant "one cat, two dogs, and a ferret."

But Emily didn't panic (much). She had a solid plan, a growing network of contractors who answered her calls even when she was in full crisis mode, and a property manager who was worth their weight in gold.

The Big Leap: Going National

After building a solid base in her hometown, Emily decided it was time to think bigger. Why limit herself to one city when there was an entire country full of potential investments? She started researching out-of-state markets like a detective on a hot case. She found areas where property values were rising, rental demand was high, and most importantly, where she could get a great deal.

Emily's first out-of-state purchase was a charming little single-family home in a suburb that was just starting to get some buzz. She flew out, toured the property, and closed the deal in record time. The local market was so different from what she was used to, but she quickly adapted, learning the ins and outs of managing from afar. And it paid off—the place was rented out within a week of closing, and the cash flow was enough to make her start looking at properties in the next state over.

The Payoff: From Small-Time Investor to Real Estate Mogul

Fast forward a few years, and Emily is the proud owner of 12 properties across four states. Her portfolio includes everything from single-family homes to small apartment buildings, each one a carefully chosen piece of her growing empire. She's got the income, the equity, and the freedom to do what she wants—whether that's scouting for new deals or finally taking that vacation she's been dreaming about.

But here's the best part: Emily built her portfolio without losing her mind (well, not completely). She learned from every challenge, adapted her strategies as she grew, and never lost sight of her ultimate goal. And now, when people ask her how she did it, she just smiles and says, "One questionable fixer-upper at a time."

The Moral of the Story: Dream Big, Start Small, and Keep Going

Emily's journey from that first shaky duplex to a multi-state portfolio is a lesson in perseverance, smart investing, and knowing when to call in the pros. She didn't rush—she strategized. She didn't just buy properties—she built a portfolio that works for her. And if Emily can do it, so can you. Just remember: every empire starts with that first creaky, slightly smelly property.

LONG-TERM VISION: PLANNING FOR FUTURE **SUCCESS**

Alright, let's get real for a second. You didn't get into real estate just to make a quick buck, did you? Sure, flipping a house or two is fun—like redecorating your living room, but with a bigger paycheck at the end. But if you want to stay in the game, build wealth, and one day buy that private island you've been eyeing on Zillow (yes, that's a thing), you need a long-term vision.

Planning for future success in real estate isn't just about having a stack of properties and waiting for the money to roll in. It's about strategy, foresight, and making decisions now that your future self will high-five you for later. So let's dive into how you can set yourself up for the kind of success that has people asking, "How did they do it?"

Think Big, Start Small, and Plan to Dominate

First things first: You need to think big. I'm talking "taking over the world, Pinky and the Brain" big. But here's the kicker—start small. That first single-family home you bought? It's just the beginning. Your long-term vision should be about expanding, scaling, and building something that lasts.

- **Set Your Goals:** Where do you want to be in five, ten, or twenty years? Are you looking to retire early, build a legacy, or just own enough properties to wallpaper your office with deeds? Write down your goals, stick them somewhere visible, and let them guide every move you make.

- **Plan for Growth:** Don't just buy properties—buy strategically. Think about how each property fits into your overall plan. Will it appreciate over time? Will it generate steady cash flow? Can you leverage it to buy more properties? Each purchase should be a stepping stone toward your bigger picture.

- **Play the Long Game:** Real estate is not a sprint; it's a marathon that sometimes feels like an obstacle course. You'll have ups, downs, and the occasional tenant who thinks paying rent is optional. Keep your eyes on the prize and don't get sidetracked by short-term distractions.

Diversify Like a Pro

You've heard the saying, "Don't put all your eggs in one basket," right? In real estate, that's not just advice—it's a survival strategy. Diversification is your secret weapon against market fluctuations, tenant troubles, and that one property that just refuses to sell.

- **Mix It Up:** Own some residential properties, a few commercial spaces, maybe even a vacation rental or two. Different types of properties perform differently under various market conditions, so having a mix means you're protected no matter what.

- **Geographic Spread:** Don't limit yourself to one market. If all your properties are in one city and that city's market tanks, you're in trouble. Invest in different areas, maybe even different states. This way, if one market dips, another might be booming.

- **Consider REITs:** If you want to diversify even further without buying more physical properties, consider real estate investment trusts (REITs). They let you invest in real estate portfolios and spread your risk without having to deal with tenants or toilets.

Future-Proof Your Investments

The real estate market is like the weather—always changing, sometimes unpredictable, and often requiring an umbrella (metaphorically speaking). To stay ahead, you need to future-proof your investments.

- **Stay Ahead of Trends:** Pay attention to market trends, economic indicators, and demographic shifts. Is there a new tech hub popping up? Are millennials moving to the suburbs? Use this information to make informed decisions about where and what to invest in next.

- **Upgrade Your Properties:** Don't let your investments get outdated. Keep up with maintenance, make necessary upgrades, and consider adding features that appeal to modern tenants, like energy-efficient appliances or smart home technology. Properties that evolve with the times are the ones that stay valuable.

- **Plan for Market Shifts:** The market will go up, and the market will go down. It's the circle of life, real estate edition. Plan for it. Have a rainy-day fund, know when to hold 'em, know when to fold 'em (thanks, Kenny Rogers), and be ready to pivot when the market takes a turn.

Build Your Dream Team

No real estate mogul does it alone. Behind every successful investor is a team of experts who make sure everything runs smoothly while you're out there making deals and looking good doing it.

- **The Right Agent:** Your real estate agent is your partner in crime, your deal-finding dynamo. They know the market, they know the players, and they know how to negotiate like a boss. Find someone who gets your vision and is as committed to your success as you are.

- **A Killer Accountant:** Taxes are a big deal in real estate, and the last thing you want is to get tripped up by the IRS. Get an accountant who knows the ins and outs of real estate investing, someone who can help you maximize deductions, defer taxes, and keep Uncle Sam happy.

- **Reliable Contractors:** Your properties are only as good as the people who maintain them. Build relationships with contractors you trust, who show up on time, do quality work, and don't charge you an arm and a leg.

- **A Great Property Manager:** If you've got more properties than you have time (and that's the goal), a property manager is essential. They handle the day-to-day stuff, so you can focus on growing your empire.

Legacy Planning: Because You Can't Take It With You

Let's get real—eventually, all of us are going to hang up our keys. What happens to your real estate empire then? Legacy planning is the final piece of the puzzle, ensuring that all your hard work benefits the next generation (or at least funds a really cool monument in your honor).

- **Estate Planning:** Work with an estate planner to ensure your properties are passed on according to your wishes, with minimal taxes and legal hassles. This is about making sure your legacy isn't just a mess of probate court and unhappy heirs.

Create a Trust: Consider setting up a real estate trust to manage your properties after you're gone. Trusts can provide stability, ensure your properties are managed according to your wishes, and protect your assets from being squandered.

- **Teach the Next Generation:** If you're planning to pass your portfolio on to your kids or grandkids, start teaching them the ropes now. Share your knowledge, involve them in the business, and instill the values that made you successful. That way, your empire continues to thrive long after you're gone.

The Future is Yours—Plan Like It

Building a real estate empire isn't just about what you do today; it's about what you set up for tomorrow. Your long-term vision is the roadmap that guides every decision, every investment, and every move you make in this industry. It's about playing chess while everyone else is playing checkers—always thinking three steps ahead, always planning for the next big thing.

So, dream big, plan smart, and stay focused on the future. Because when you've got a clear vision and a solid plan, there's nothing that can stop you from building the real estate empire of your dreams. And who knows? Maybe one day, that private island will be more than just a Zillow fantasy.

The Long Game Legend: How Jake Built a Real Estate Empire One Smart Move at a Time

Jake, who took the idea of long-term vision and turned it into a real estate masterclass. Jake didn't just want to dip his toes into real estate; he wanted to cannonball into the deep end and make waves. But here's the thing about Jake—he wasn't in a hurry. He knew from day one that building an empire takes time, patience, and a plan so solid you could build a skyscraper on it.

The Slow and Steady Start

Jake started his journey like most investors—buying a single-family home in a neighborhood that was "on the rise." You know the type: a place where the local coffee shop is still deciding whether it wants to serve artisan lattes or just stick with the burnt drip coffee. Jake saw potential where others saw peeling paint and overgrown lawns.

But here's where Jake was different. While his friends were flipping properties faster than you can say "HGTV," Jake held onto that house like it was his golden ticket. And you know what? He was right. Over the next few years, as the neighborhood transformed from "up-and-coming" to "trendy and untouchable," the value of Jake's little house skyrocketed.

The "Boring" Expansion

Now, most people would take that appreciation and cash out, but not Jake. No, Jake had a vision—a vision that required patience, discipline, and a love for what he called "boring investments." You see, Jake wasn't interested in the flashiest properties or the biggest immediate returns. He was all about steady, reliable growth.

Jake started buying up small multifamily properties in stable, middle-class neighborhoods. These weren't the kind of places that made the front page of the real estate section, but they were consistent. The rent checks came in on time, the tenants stayed for years, and the properties appreciated slowly but surely.

The "Future-Proof" Strategy

Jake had one rule: every property he bought had to be future-proof. What does that mean? It means Jake didn't just look at what a property could do for him today; he looked at what it could do for him ten, twenty, even thirty years down the line.

- **Neighborhood Trends:** Jake became an expert at spotting neighborhoods that were poised for long-term growth. He didn't chase the latest hot spot; he invested in places with good schools, solid infrastructure, and potential for future development. When the big investors finally showed up, Jake was already there, sipping his coffee and watching his property values climb.

- **Low Maintenance, High Return:** Jake wasn't about to spend his weekends fixing leaky faucets or replacing roofs. He invested in properties that were low-maintenance and reliable. If it didn't have good bones, it wasn't getting into Jake's portfolio.

- **Smart Upgrades:** While others were installing gold-plated faucets, Jake focused on smart, future-proof upgrades like energy-efficient appliances, solar panels, and sustainable landscaping. These weren't just trendy; they were investments that would pay off in the long run.

The "Legacy" Move

Jake wasn't just thinking about his retirement; he was thinking about his kids' and grandkids' future. He wanted to build something that would last —a legacy. So, when the time came, Jake started working with an estate planner. He set up trusts for each of his properties, ensuring they would be passed down smoothly, without the usual family drama (we've all seen Succession, right?).

But Jake didn't stop there. He made sure his kids were in the loop. Every family dinner turned into a mini real estate seminar, with Jake sharing his strategies, his successes, and, yes, even his failures. By the time his kids were old enough to take the reins, they were ready—not just to maintain Jake's portfolio, but to grow it.

The Payoff

Fast forward a couple of decades, and Jake is living the dream. His portfolio has grown exponentially, his properties are all but printing money, and his kids are carrying on the family business. Jake's long-term vision paid off in spades. He's not just a real estate investor; he's a real estate legend in his own right.

And the best part? Jake did it his way—slow, steady, and with an eye always on the future. While others chased quick wins, Jake played the long game, and it paid off big time.

The Moral of the Story

Jake's story is proof that in real estate, the tortoise really does beat the hare. By sticking to his vision, making smart, future-proof investments, and thinking not just about today but about tomorrow and beyond, Jake built a real estate empire that will last for generations.

So, take a page out of Jake's book. Dream big, plan for the long haul, and remember: slow and steady not only wins the race but also builds the kind of wealth that lets you retire on a beach somewhere far, far away—preferably with a piña colada in hand.

REFLECTING ON THE JOURNEY: LESSONS LEARNED AND **NEXT STEPS**

Alright, let's take a moment to step back and reflect on this wild ride called real estate investing. You've been through the ups and downs, the highs and lows, and probably a few moments where you questioned your sanity. But here you are —wiser, wealthier (hopefully), and with a story or two that you can share at dinner parties to make everyone else feel like they need to get their lives together.

Real estate isn't just about buying and selling properties; it's a journey of growth, learning, and, let's be honest, a fair amount of winging it. So, what have we learned along the way, and where do we go from here? Let's dive into the lessons you've picked up and the steps you should take as you continue your journey to real estate greatness.

The Power of Patience: Slow and Steady Wins the Race

If there's one thing you've probably realized by now, it's that real estate is not a get-rich-quick scheme. Sure, the TV shows make it look like you can flip a house in a weekend and retire by Tuesday, but the reality? It's more like a long game of chess, where each move counts and sometimes you've got to wait for the right moment to strike.

- **Lesson Learned:** Patience pays off. Whether it's waiting for the market to turn, tenants to mature, or that perfect property to come along, the real winners in real estate are those who play the long game.

- **Next Step:** Keep your cool. Don't rush into decisions because you feel pressured or impatient. Remember, real estate is a marathon, not a sprint. Your next big opportunity is just around the corner—stay ready.

Embrace the Unexpected: Flexibility is Key

Remember that time the market tanked just after you bought that "can't-miss" property? Or when your tenants decided to redecorate by flooding the kitchen? Yeah, real estate has a funny way of throwing curveballs when you least expect it. But here's the thing: the best investors aren't the ones who avoid challenges—they're the ones who adapt.

- **Lesson Learned:** Flexibility is your best friend. Whether it's pivoting your strategy, adjusting your expectations, or just rolling with the punches, the ability to adapt is what keeps you in the game.

- **Next Step:** Stay nimble. Keep learning, keep adjusting, and always be ready to pivot if the situation calls for it. The market changes, people change, and you should be ready to change too.

The Importance of Relationships: People Matter

In real estate, it's easy to get caught up in the numbers, but at the end of the day, it's the people who make or break your success. From your real estate agent to your contractors, your tenants to your lenders—relationships are the backbone of your business.

- **Lesson Learned:** Building and maintaining strong relationships is essential. Trustworthy partners, reliable tenants, and good rapport with everyone involved can turn a good investment into a great one.
- **Next Step:** Cultivate your network. Keep in touch with your key contacts, treat your tenants well, and always be on the lookout for new relationships that can help you grow your business.

Knowledge is Power: Stay Educated

If you've made it this far, you've probably learned a thing or two about the real estate world. But here's the kicker—there's always more to learn. The market is constantly evolving, new trends emerge, and regulations change. Staying on top of these developments is crucial to staying ahead.

- **Lesson Learned:** Never stop learning. The most successful investors are those who continuously seek out new knowledge, whether it's through books, seminars, or good old-fashioned experience.
- **Next Step:** Commit to ongoing education. Set aside time each week to learn something new about real estate— whether it's market trends, investment strategies, or tax tips. The more you know, the better equipped you are to make smart decisions.

Celebrate the Wins, Learn from the Losses

Let's be real—there have been some amazing highs and some pretty low lows along this journey. Maybe you scored a killer deal on a property that tripled in value, or maybe you had a flip that turned into a flop. But every experience, good or bad, has something to teach you.

- **Lesson Learned:** Success in real estate is about more than just the wins. It's about learning from every experience, whether it's a victory or a setback.

- **Next Step:** Reflect on your journey. Take time to review your successes and your mistakes. Celebrate your achievements (because you deserve it), and identify areas where you can improve. Use these insights to shape your future strategies.

Planning for the Future: What's Next?

So, you've built a portfolio, navigated some challenges, and picked up a ton of knowledge along the way. What now? This is where your long-term vision really comes into play. It's time to think about where you want to go next and how you're going to get there.

- **Lesson Learned:** The journey never really ends. There's always another deal, another challenge, another opportunity. But with the right vision and strategy, you can keep moving forward and growing your wealth.

- **Next Step:** Set new goals. Whether it's expanding your portfolio, diversifying into new markets, or finally taking that vacation you've been dreaming about, it's time to plan your next move. Keep your long-term vision in mind, and start laying the groundwork for your next chapter.

The Journey Continues

Reflecting on your real estate journey is more than just a trip down memory lane—it's about recognizing how far you've come and using that knowledge to propel yourself forward. You've navigated challenges, learned invaluable lessons, and built something truly impressive. But the best part? You're just getting started.

So, take a moment to appreciate the journey so far, but don't get too comfortable. The real estate world is full of new opportunities, and your next big success could be just around the corner. Keep learning, keep growing, and most importantly, keep having fun—because in real estate, the journey is as exciting as the destination.

Sarah's Reflection: How Pausing and Planning Turned a Real Estate Hustle into a Lasting Legacy

Alright, let's take a moment to step back and reflect on this wild ride called real estate investing. You've been through the ups and downs, the highs and lows, and probably a few moments where you questioned your sanity. But here you are—wiser, wealthier (hopefully), and with a story or two that you can share at dinner parties to make everyone else feel like they need to get their lives together.

Real estate isn't just about buying and selling properties; it's a journey of growth, learning, and, let's be honest, a fair amount of winging it. So, what have we learned along the way, and where do we go from here? Let's dive into the lessons you've picked up and the steps you should take as you continue your journey to real estate greatness.

The Power of Patience: Slow and Steady Wins the Race

If there's one thing you've probably realized by now, it's that real estate is not a get-rich-quick scheme. Sure, the TV shows make it look like you can flip a house in a weekend and retire by Tuesday, but the reality? It's more like a long game of chess, where each move counts and sometimes you've got to wait for the right moment to strike.

- **Lesson Learned:** Patience pays off. Whether it's waiting for the market to turn, tenants to mature, or that perfect property to come along, the real winners in real estate are those who play the long game.

- **Next Step:** Keep your cool. Don't rush into decisions because you feel pressured or impatient. Remember, real estate is a marathon, not a sprint. Your next big opportunity is just around the corner—stay ready.

Embrace the Unexpected: Flexibility is Key

Remember that time the market tanked just after you bought that "can't-miss" property? Or when your tenants decided to redecorate by flooding the kitchen? Yeah, real estate has a funny way of throwing curveballs when you least expect it. But here's the thing: the best investors aren't the ones who avoid challenges—they're the ones who adapt.

- **Lesson Learned:** Flexibility is your best friend. Whether it's pivoting your strategy, adjusting your expectations, or just rolling with the punches, the ability to adapt is what keeps you in the game.
- **Next Step:** Stay nimble. Keep learning, keep adjusting, and always be ready to pivot if the situation calls for it. The market changes, people change, and you should be ready to change too.

The Importance of Relationships: People Matter

In real estate, it's easy to get caught up in the numbers, but at the end of the day, it's the people who make or break your success. From your real estate agent to your contractors, your tenants to your lenders—relationships are the backbone of your business.

- **Lesson Learned:** Building and maintaining strong relationships is essential. Trustworthy partners, reliable tenants, and good rapport with everyone involved can turn a good investment into a great one.
- **Next Step:** Cultivate your network. Keep in touch with your key contacts, treat your tenants well, and always be on the lookout for new relationships that can help you grow your business.

Knowledge is Power: Stay Educated

If you've made it this far, you've probably learned a thing or two about the real estate world. But here's the kicker—there's always more to learn. The market is constantly evolving, new trends emerge, and regulations change. Staying on top of these developments is crucial to staying ahead.

- **Lesson Learned:** Never stop learning. The most successful investors are those who continuously seek out new knowledge, whether it's through books, seminars, or good old-fashioned experience.
- **Next Step:** Commit to ongoing education. Set aside time each week to learn something new about real estate—whether it's market trends, investment strategies, or tax tips. The more you know, the better equipped you are to make smart decisions.

Celebrate the Wins, Learn from the Losses

Let's be real—there have been some amazing highs and some pretty low lows along this journey. Maybe you scored a killer deal on a property that tripled in value, or maybe you had a flip that turned into a flop. But every experience, good or bad, has something to teach you.

- **Lesson Learned:** Success in real estate is about more than just the wins. It's about learning from every experience, whether it's a victory or a setback.
- **Next Step:** Reflect on your journey. Take time to review your successes and your mistakes. Celebrate your achievements (because you deserve it), and identify areas where you can improve. Use these insights to shape your future strategies.

Planning for the Future: What's Next?

So, you've built a portfolio, navigated some challenges, and picked up a ton of knowledge along the way. What now? This is where your long-term vision really comes into play. It's time to think about where you want to go next and how you're going to get there.

- Lesson Learned: The journey never really ends. There's always another deal, another challenge, another opportunity. But with the right vision and strategy, you can keep moving forward and growing your wealth.
- Next Step: Set new goals. Whether it's expanding your portfolio, diversifying into new markets, or finally taking that vacation you've been dreaming about, it's time to plan your next move. Keep your long-term vision in mind, and start laying the groundwork for your next chapter.

The Journey Continues

Reflecting on your real estate journey is more than just a trip down memory lane—it's about recognizing how far you've come and using that knowledge to propel yourself forward. You've navigated challenges, learned invaluable lessons, and built something truly impressive. But the best part? You're just getting started.

So, take a moment to appreciate the journey so far, but don't get too comfortable. The real estate world is full of new opportunities, and your next big success could be just around the corner. Keep learning, keep growing, and most importantly, keep having fun—because in real estate, the journey is as exciting as the destination.

THE JOURNEY CONTINUES: YOUR NEXT STEPS IN **REAL ESTATE SUCCESS**

Alright, let's take a moment to savor this—because if you're reading this, you've made it to the end of one heck of a ride. You've been through the trenches of tenant troubles, survived the stress of closing deals, and maybe even dodged a few leaky roofs along the way. But let's be real—this isn't the finish line. Oh no, my friend, this is just the beginning of your real estate rockstar journey.

You didn't come this far just to come this far, right? Whether you're a seasoned pro or you're still trying to figure out why your first property smells like wet socks, the adventure is just getting started. So let's talk about what comes next. Spoiler alert: it involves you being awesome, making money, and maybe even taking over the world—one property at a time.

Keep Your Eyes on the Prize: The Infinite Game

Let's get one thing straight—real estate is not a Netflix binge. There's no satisfying series finale where everything wraps up neatly. This is an infinite game, my friend, where the only goal is to keep playing, keep winning, and keep growing.

- **New Goals, Who Dis?** You've crushed some goals, but now it's time to set new ones. Whether it's buying that dream penthouse or expanding into commercial properties, keep those goals fresh and ambitious.

- **Stay Hungry, Stay Foolish:** Steve Jobs said it best, but it applies to real estate too. Stay curious, stay motivated, and never lose that fire that got you into this crazy game in the first place.

- **Pace Yourself:** Real estate is more of a marathon with a few sprints thrown in, not a 100-meter dash. There will be times when you're flying high and times when you feel like you're stuck in the mud. Keep moving, and you'll come out on top.

Innovate or Get Left Behind: Be Ready for What's Next

The only constant in real estate? Change. The market shifts, new technologies emerge, and suddenly everyone's talking about NFTs when you just figured out Airbnb. Stay ahead by being the investor who's always ready for what's next.

- **Tech it to the Next Level:** Get cozy with tech. Virtual tours, AI-driven analytics, apps that make your life easier—embrace it all. It's not just for the cool kids; it's for smart investors who want to stay ahead of the curve.

- **Flexibility is Your Superpower:** Don't be that investor stuck in their ways. Be ready to pivot, adapt, and change course when the market throws you a curveball. Because it will. And when it does, you'll be ready.

- **Think Big, Stay Creative:** Don't just follow the crowd. Be the one who sees opportunity where others see obstacles. That weird little property no one wants? It could be your next goldmine. Think outside the box and reap the rewards.

Your Network is Your Net Worth: Build and Nurture Relationships

You've probably heard it a million times, but it's true: in real estate, it's not just about what you know, it's about who you know. So keep building those relationships and treating people right. It'll pay off big time.

- **BFFs with Your Real Estate Agent:** Your agent isn't just someone who opens doors and hands you keys. They're your partner in crime, your deal-making confidante. Keep them close, and they'll keep bringing you those sweet deals.

- **The Magic of Mentorship:** Pay it forward. Be a mentor, find a mentor, or better yet, do both. Teaching others not only helps them but also reminds you of how far you've come.

- **Tenants are People Too:** Yes, they pay your bills, but they're also human beings. Treat them well, and they'll take care of your properties. And when they move on, they'll recommend you to others.

Legacy Building: Because You Can't Take It with You

Let's face it—at some point, you're going to want to kick back, relax, and maybe even hand the reins over to the next generation. But how do you make sure everything you've built doesn't crumble the minute you step back?

- **Plan Like a Pro:** Get your estate in order. Wills, trusts, all that grown-up stuff you've been avoiding? Yeah, time to handle it. Make sure your empire is protected and ready to be passed down smoothly.

- **Teach the Next Gen:** Whether it's your kids, nieces, nephews, or that protégé you took under your wing, start sharing your knowledge now. Real estate wisdom is the gift that keeps on giving.

- **Leave a Mark:** Think about how you want to be remembered. Maybe it's through a foundation, a scholarship, or just being known as the investor who made a positive impact on the community. Whatever it is, start building that legacy now.

Don't Forget to Have Fun: Celebrate the Wins

Look, real estate can be intense, but it should also be fun. You didn't work this hard just to stress yourself out, right? Enjoy the journey, celebrate the victories, and laugh off the setbacks. You've earned it.

- **Pop Some Champagne:** Closed a big deal? Hit a milestone? Take a moment to celebrate. Go out, have fun, treat yourself. You deserve it.

- **Take a Breather:** Every now and then, step back and recharge. Whether it's a weekend getaway or just a day off to binge-watch something completely unrelated to real estate, make time for yourself.

- **Remember the Why:** Why did you get into real estate in the first place? Keep that at the forefront, and it'll make even the tough days worth it.

The Journey is Just Getting Started

You've come a long way, but trust me—the best is yet to come. The deals, the growth, the success—it's all within your reach. So keep learning, keep hustling, and keep dreaming big. Because in real estate, there's always another adventure just around the corner.

This isn't the end of your story; it's just the beginning of an epic saga. So go out there, take on the world, and show everyone what you're made of. You've got this. And who knows? Maybe one day, we'll be reading about you in the next great real estate success story.

APPENDIX: RESOURCES AND TOOLS FOR REAL ESTATE PROFESSIONALS

Navigating the real estate industry requires access to the right resources and tools. This appendix provides a comprehensive list of valuable resources to help you stay informed, enhance your skills, and leverage technology effectively. Whether you're a seasoned professional or just starting out, these resources will support your journey towards excellence.

Real Estate Investment Tools

Property Analysis Software

- **DealCheck:** A comprehensive tool for analyzing potential deals, calculating returns, and running scenarios.
- **Roofstock:** Great for evaluating single-family rental properties, especially if you're looking to invest remotely.

Property Management Software

- **Buildium:** Ideal for managing rental properties, handling tenant communication, and streamlining maintenance requests.
- **AppFolio:** A full-suite property management platform with robust features for larger portfolios.

Mortgage Calculators

- **Bankrate Mortgage Calculator:** Useful for calculating monthly payments, comparing loan offers, and understanding the impact of different interest rates.

- **Zillow Mortgage Calculator:** Helps you estimate your monthly mortgage payments, including taxes and insurance.

Educational Resources

Books

- **"Rich Dad Poor Dad" by Robert Kiyosaki:** A classic read for understanding the fundamentals of wealth-building through real estate.

- **"The Millionaire Real Estate Investor" by Gary Keller:** Offers insights into building a real estate portfolio and achieving financial independence.

- **"The Book on Rental Property Investing" by Brandon Turner:** A comprehensive guide to becoming a successful rental property investor.

Podcasts

- **BiggerPockets Real Estate Podcast:** Packed with interviews, tips, and stories from successful investors, this podcast is a must-listen for anyone serious about real estate.

- **The Real Estate Guys Radio Show:** Offers expert advice on investing in real estate, with a focus on market trends and strategies.

- **Real Estate Investing for Cash Flow:** Focuses on commercial real estate and multifamily investments, providing deep dives into these areas.

Websites

- **BiggerPockets.com:** A comprehensive resource with forums, guides, calculators, and more to help you learn and grow as a real estate investor.

- **Investopedia Real Estate Investing:** Offers educational articles and guides on various aspects of real estate investing.

Networking and Mentorship

Real Estate Investment Groups (REIGs)

- **Local REIGs:** Join a local real estate investment group to network with other investors, learn about local market trends, and find potential deals.

- **National REIGs:** Consider joining national groups like the National Real Estate Investors Association (NREIA) for broader networking opportunities and resources.

Mentorship Programs

- **BiggerPockets Mentorship:** Connect with experienced investors who can guide you through the complexities of real estate investing.

- **Local Mentorship:** Look for experienced investors in your area who offer mentorship services or are open to informal mentoring relationships.

Legal and Financial Resources

Real Estate Attorneys

- **Find a Local Attorney:** Always have a trusted real estate attorney on hand for reviewing contracts, handling disputes, and navigating legal complexities.

- **American Bar Association:** Use the ABA's lawyer directory to find a qualified real estate attorney in your area.

Accountants and CPAs

- **Real Estate-Specific CPAs:** Look for accountants who specialize in real estate to help you navigate tax strategies, deductions, and financial planning.
- **The National Society of Accountants:** Use their directory to find CPAs and accountants who can help manage your real estate finances.

Insurance Providers

- **Landlord Insurance:** Make sure you're properly covered with landlord insurance, which protects you from potential risks associated with renting out properties.
- **Umbrella Insurance:** Consider an umbrella policy to provide additional liability coverage beyond your standard property insurance.

Tips for Success

- **Start with a Plan:** Before making any investments, create a detailed business plan outlining your goals, strategies, and financial projections.
- **Do Your Due Diligence:** Always conduct thorough due diligence on any property you're considering, including market research, property inspections, and financial analysis.
- **Stay Educated:** The real estate market is always changing. Stay informed by continuously educating yourself on new trends, laws, and strategies.
- **Build a Strong Team:** Surround yourself with a reliable team of professionals, including agents, attorneys, accountants, and property managers.

- **Be Patient:** Real estate success doesn't happen overnight. Stay patient, stick to your plan, and make informed decisions to build long-term wealth.

ACKNOWLEDGMENTS

Creating this book has been an incredible journey, and it would not have been possible without the support and contributions of many wonderful individuals.

First and foremost, I want to thank my family for their unwavering support and encouragement. Your love and belief in me have been my greatest source of strength and inspiration. To my wife, whose patience and understanding during the long hours of writing and research have been invaluable – thank you for being my rock.

I extend my heartfelt gratitude to my friends and colleagues in the real estate industry. Your insights, experiences, and advice have enriched this book in countless ways. Special thanks to my mentors, whose wisdom and guidance have shaped my career and understanding of real estate. Your influence is evident on every page of this book.

A sincere thank you to the many clients I've had the privilege to serve over the years. Your trust in me has been both an honor and a motivation to strive for excellence. The stories and experiences we've shared have greatly informed the practical advice in this book.

To the experts and authors whose works have inspired and informed my own – thank you for your contributions to the field of real estate. Your dedication to knowledge and education has provided a solid foundation upon which this book is built.

I also want to acknowledge the incredible support of my editorial and publishing team. Your expertise, feedback, and attention to detail have been crucial in shaping this book into what it is today. Thank you for believing in this project and helping to bring it to life.

Lastly, I am grateful to my readers. Your quest for knowledge and excellence in real estate is the driving force behind this book. I hope it serves as a valuable resource on your journey to success.

To everyone who has been a part of this journey – thank you. Your support, encouragement, and belief in the pursuit of excellence have made this book possible.

MEET THE **AUTHOR**

Lorenzo Sellers is Amazon's #1 Bestselling author and the founder of The SELLERS Team®, a real estate team specializing in the field of marketing homes ranging from residential to luxury and teaching first time home buyers how to effectively search for and procure the home they want.

For the past 13 years, Lorenzo has immersed himself in the intricate world of real estate marketing, collaborating with hundreds of esteemed agents and facilitating transactions totaling over $51.4 billion across California.

His approach, honed under the mentorship of industry luminaries, blends directness, transparency, sophisticated home staging, and compelling listing strategies. Expert negotiation prowess and a steadfast ability to manage both people and transactions with calm professionalism are his hallmarks. His capability is a blend of innate instinct and a steadfast commitment to continuous advanced education and training.

In 2022, upon obtaining his license, he embarked on his official real estate journey by affiliating with Keller Williams Town Center, a premier brokerage in the esteemed Hampton Roads region. Recognized among peers as an authoritative figure and prolific author in social media and digital marketing, he continuously innovates at the forefront, seamlessly integrating luxury home styling with cutting-edge technology and progressive strategies.

www.ingramcontent.com/pod-product-compliance
Lightning Source LLC
Chambersburg PA
CBHW052159220526
45471CB00004B/1735